52 HYMN STORIES
Dramatized

Books by Kenneth W. Osbeck
(published by Kregel Publications)

Amazing Grace: 366 Hymn Stories for Personal Devotions
Devotional Warm-ups for the Church Choir
52 Bible Characters Dramatized
52 Hymn Stories Dramatized
The Ministry of Music
My Music Workbook
101 Hymn Stories
101 More Hymn Stories
Pocket Guide for the Church Choir Member

52 HYMN STORIES *Dramatized*

Kenneth W. Osbeck

kregel
PUBLICATIONS

Grand Rapids, MI 49501

52 Hymn Stories Dramatized by Kenneth W. Osbeck
Copyright © 1992 by Kregel Publications, P.O. Box 2607,
Grand Rapids, Michigan 49501. All rights reserved.

Cover photo: Art Jacobs
Cover and book design: Alan G. Hartman

Library of Congress Cataloging-in-Publication Data

Osbeck, Kenneth W.
   52 Hymn Stories Dramatized / Kenneth W. Osbeck.
      p.   cm.
   1. Hymns, English. 2. Drama in Christian education.
3. Drama in public worship I. Title. II. Title: Fifty-two
hymn stories dramatized
BV315.069   1992   264'.2—dc20   91-39320
                                        CIP

ISBN 0-8254-3428-9

         4 5 6 7 8 printing/year 99 98 97 96

Printed in the United States of America

Contents

Preface

As a result of the sixteenth century Protestant Reformation, singing by the laity was restored. Since that time, evangelical leaders have realized that the most important form of musical expression in the local church is congregational singing. It is one of the finest demonstrations of a basic tenet of New Testament and Reformation teaching: *the priesthood of all believers*. This implies that each believer is an active participant rather than a mere spectator in a worship service. As ritual and pageantry have characterized, throughout history, the more liturgical churches, so vibrant singing by the lay people has been a hallmark of evangelical worship.

Yet in many churches today, congregational singing is one of the weakest activities. Often the praise time evolves into an experience of apathetic endurance or frothy emotionalism. It is tragic that many of God's people can spend a lifetime in church services and seldom realize the spiritual refreshment that results from responding to God with a "sacrifice of praise" offering (Hebrews 13:15, 16). Instead of anticipating the Lord's Day as a time of entering into His courts with joy and thanksgiving, some view it merely as another legalistic duty or a time for light-hearted religious entertainment.

The Bible contains more than 575 references to praise, music and singing. Christians have always been and will continue to be *praising people*. Sacred song is the natural out-pouring of joyous, transformed lives. The song of praise that began at creation (Job 38:7) will continue throughout eternity. There is still no lovelier sound than the united voices of a congregation lifting joyful praise to their Lord.

Passages such as these give a strong plea for inspirational, thoughtful singing in our corporate worship:

> "Speak to one another with psalms, hymns and spiritual songs. Sing and make music in your heart to the Lord, always giving thanks to God the Father for everything, in the name of our Lord Jesus Christ."   *Ephesians 5:19, 20*

"Let the word of Christ dwell in you richly as you teach and admonish (encourage) one another with all wisdom, and as you sing psalms, hymns and spiritual songs with gratitude in your hearts to God."
Colossians 3:16

". . . in the presence of the congregation I will sing Your praises."   *Hebrews 2:12*

The purpose of these dramatic hymn sketches is to encourage God's people to rediscover joyful and edifying singing in the church, fulfilling the scriptural directive—"sing with the spirit, but also sing with the mind" (1 Corinthians 14:15).

With these brief sketches a song/worship leader can frequently feature (even weekly) a particular hymn with an interesting and informative presentation of its origin and meaning. In this way a leader can enhance the congregation's appreciation for their hymnal—*a most important heritage of the Christian church*—and can also involve others more actively in the service.

May we as God's *praising people* respond with genuine joy and understanding whenever there is opportunity. May our times of worship always be characterized with psalms, hymns and spiritual songs that truly exalt the Lord, encourage one another, and enrich our own spiritual lives.

"Come, Christians, join to sing—Alleluia! Amen.
Loud praise to Christ our King—Alleluia! Amen.
Let all with heart and voice, before His throne rejoice;
Praise is His gracious choice: Alleluia! Amen!"
—Christian Henry Bateman

KEN OSBECK

Unless otherwise indicated, Scripture quotations are from the *Holy Bible,* New International Version, copyright 1973, 1978, 1984 by the International Bible Society. Used by permission of Zondervan Bible Publishers.

Further Suggestions

These dramatic sketches can be given as simply or elaborately as desired. The parts can merely be read or they could be memorized and presented with costumes and props. The important object is to inspire people to sing and understand these hymns with greater appreciation. There should be a genuine effort to involve creatively the congregation, singing groups or soloists in presenting the hymns profiled in this collection.

It might also be helpful to include in the church bulletin a few brief lines about the hymn and its main characters whenever these sketches are featured in a service. For more complete information about each hymn, note the pages listed that refer to our books, *101* and *101 More Hymn Stories*.

A Mighty Fortress Is Our God

3 Characters: 2 Readers, Martin Luther

Reader 1:   If you and I had been living in the city of Wittenberg (VIT-ten-berg), Germany, on October 31, 1517, we might have heard a sound similar to this:

(Pounding with a hammer)

Reader 2:   This pounding was heard at the doors of the beautiful Wittenberg Cathedral on the day that Martin Luther, an Augustinian monk and professor of theology at the university, posted a list of 95 complaints against many of the established teachings and practices of the Roman Church. And with this proclamation of Luther's 95 Theses, the sixteenth century Protestant Reformation Movement was formally born.

Martin Luther: "Recently here at the University of Wittenberg, while studying the Scriptures earnestly, especially the Books of Romans and Galatians, I have become increasingly impressed with the truth of the priesthood of each believer. It grieves me deeply that the church has long deprived our lay people from going directly to God by simply responding in personal faith to the finished work of Christ. For centuries now these devout folks have been taught the shameful lie that the Almighty could only be approached through the prescribed rituals, practices and sacraments of the church—administered by those priests."

Reader 1:   Another practice of the church that greatly disturbed Martin Luther was the selling of papal indulgences to the lay people. This was done at that time for the purpose of collecting funds to rebuild the magnificent St. Peter's Church in the Vatican at Rome.

Reader 2:   With the purchase of these little pieces of paper, the people were assured by their leaders that sins would be forgiven and that loved ones would be freed sooner from purgatory.

Martin Luther: "When I heard for myself that rascal priest, John Tetzel (TETZ-el), tell our people—'as soon as your coin clinks in this chest, the souls of your loved ones will rise out of purgatory into heaven'—I was horrified and could keep silent no longer. I prepared a list of 95 complaints against the church and posted them on the doors of our cathedral here at Wittenberg on that memorable day of October 31, 1517. Never in my wildest imagination did I foresee that my list of complaints would become the spark that would ignite the spiritual flame that has now spread throughout all of Europe."

Reader 1:   Many of the church's leaders had also insisted for some time that only they were capable of understanding and interpreting the Holy Bible properly—in Latin, of course!

Martin Luther: "I have put forth every effort to change this, by restoring God's Word once again to the lay people and translating it for them into their own language. I want the commonest person in the marketplace to read and know the Scriptures."

Reader 2:   Then the church leaders had also long decreed that since they alone could read and interpret the Bible properly, only the clergy and trained choirs should sing in church. For more than 1,000 years, the lay people had remained silent and been denied the right to raise their voices in praise to God in the worship services.

Martin Luther: "This, too, is wrong! Not only must God speak directly to each individual through His inspired Word, but we His people must respond to Him—in our own language—with joyful expressions of praise. Next to the preaching of the Scriptures themselves, I now afford music the highest place in the church. I want the Word of God to dwell in the hearts of believers by means of song. And if any person will not speak and sing of what Christ has wrought for us, he shows thereby that he does not truly believe."

Reader 1:   Since congregations had no songs to sing in their church services for so many years, Martin Luther began writing a number of them, often both words and music.

These little hymns had a powerful influence in the spread of the gospel. His many enemies often lamented—

Reader 2:   Those poor German people are singing themselves into Luther's terrible doctrines, and his hymns are destroying more souls than all of his sermons and writings combined.

Martin Luther: "I have become so convinced about the value of singing in the Christian ministry, that now I would allow no one to preach or teach God's people who does not realize and practice the power of sacred songs. I believe that the Devil, the originator of sorrowful anxieties and restless troubles, flees before the sound of sacred music almost as much as before the Word of God itself."

Reader 1:   Whenever spiritual struggles disturbed him most, Martin Luther would turn to one of his favorite portions of Scripture, Psalm 46. These words became his source of daily help and encouragement:

Reader 2:   "God is our refuge and strength, an ever-present help in trouble.
Therefore we will not fear, though the earth give way and the mountains fall into the heart of the sea,
Though its waters roar and foam and the mountains quake with their surging—
The Lord Almighty is with us; the God of Jacob is our fortress."

Martin Luther: "I have been so inspired by these words that I have written a hymn based on this text. I also adapted some familiar music for these lines. And now these musical truths have become the great rallying cry for our German people. How my soul thrills whenever I hear our people sing this hymn—in unison and with great spiritual fervor."

(Instruments play a portion of "A Mighty Fortress")

Reader 1:   This majestic hymn of the church, "A Mighty Fortress Is Our God," was written and composed by Martin Luther. Although the exact date of the hymn cannot be fixed with any exact certainty—

Reader 2:   It is generally believed to have been officially used for the Diet or Assembly of Spires in 1529, when the term "Protestant" was first introduced.

Reader 1:   And even now, more than four and a half centuries later, we respond with much enthusiasm whenever we hear and sing this historic hymn. May we always be grateful to reformers such as Martin Luther for these spiritual blessings that are ours today:

Reader 2:   (1) A clear understanding of the biblical truth that our eternal standing with God rests not on the decrees of men but solely on a personal response by faith to the redemptive work of Christ . . .

Reader 1:   (2) The opportunity to use God's inspired Holy Word in our own language for daily strength and guidance . . .

Reader 2:   (3) And the return of congregational singing to our services of worship.

Martin Luther: "Let goods and kindred go, this mortal life also—the body they may kill; God's truth abideth still: HIS KINGDOM IS FOREVER." Amen!

(Congregation sings "A Mighty Fortress")

See page 13, *101 Hymn Stories*

All Hail the Power of Jesus' Name

4 Characters: 2 Readers, Edward Perronet, Missionary E.P. Scott

Reader 1:   The featured hymn for this service has been called "the national anthem of Christendom." Others have said, "It is a hymn that will be sung as long as there are Christians on earth, and after that—throughout eternity."

Reader 2:   Since its appearance in 1779, this hymn text has become one of the truly important worship hymns of our Christian faith. It has been translated into almost every language where Christianity is known, and wherever it is sung, this hymn has a unique way of ministering to the spiritual needs of the human heart.

(Instruments play "All Hail the Power of Jesus' Name"—"Coronation" Tune)

Reader 2:   This inspiring worship hymn of the church, "All Hail the Power of Jesus' Name," was written by Edward Perronet (Per-ro-NAY), a young English minister who lived from 1726-1792.

Reader 1:   Edward Perronet was a descendant of distinguished French Huguenots (HU-ga-nots) who had fled to Switzerland and later to England because of the religious persecution in France. Edward's father, though an ordained minister in the Anglican Church of England, was strongly sympathetic with the ministry of John and Charles Wesley and the evangelical movement that was sweeping Great Britain at that time. When Edward became an Anglican minister he also was highly critical of its ways. Once he wrote—

Edward Perronet: "I was born and I am likely to die in the tottering communion of the Church of England, but I despise her nonsense."

Reader 2:   Soon, however, young Perronet broke from the state church and threw himself strenuously into the evangelistic endeavors of the Wesleys in the 1740s and 1750s.

Reader 1:   It was during this time that the Wesleys and their followers suffered much persecution and even violence from those who opposed their ministry. This notation in John Wesley's diary relates one experience involving Edward Perronet.

Reader 2:   "From Rockdale we went to Bolton, and soon found that the Rockdale lions were lambs in comparison with those of Bolton. Edward Perronet was thrown down and rolled in mud and mire. Stones were hurled and windows broken."

Reader 1:   At times this mob opposition was inflamed by the local Anglican clergymen, who would go from house to house charging that the Wesleys, with their emphasis on a personal conversion experience, were preaching blasphemy against the established state church and should be run out of town.

Reader 2:   Though life was difficult for these dissenting preachers, their converts suffered even more. They were stoned and mauled and their homes and businesses were looted. It was commonly said that anyone who walked through a town where the Wesleys had preached could pick out by their ruinous condition the homes where the Methodist followers lived.

Reader 1:   Edward Perronet eventually became the respected pastor of an independent church at Canterbury, England, until his death at the age of 66. As he lay dying, his final words were—

Edward Perronet: "Glory to God in the height of His divinity!
Glory to God in the depth of His humanity!
Glory to God in His all-sufficiency!
Into His hands I commend my spirit!"

Reader 1:   The three fine tunes that have been used with the "All Hail the Power" text have undoubtedly increased its popularity. The tune known as "Coronation" is most widely used in this country. It was composed in 1792 by an American businessman, lay preacher and musician, Oliver Holden.

Another fine tune called "Miles Lane" has been the one most commonly used in Great Britain. It sounds like this—

(Instruments play a portion of the "Miles Lane" tune)

Reader 2:   And another musical arrangement for this text which is especially popular with church choirs everywhere is the "Diadem Tune." It was composed 50 years later than the text by a 19 year old English hat maker, James Ellor. This more elaborate music is characteristic of the musical style of that period.

(Instruments play a portion of the "Diadem Tune")

Reader 1:   A pioneer missionary to India, Mr. E.P. Scott, had a remarkable experience with this hymn—

Missionary E.P. Scott: "One day I was waylaid by a murderous band of tribesmen who were closing in on me with spears. On impulse I took my violin out of my luggage, closed my eyes and began to play and sing 'All Hail the Power of Jesus' Name.' When I reached the stanza— 'Let every kindred, every tribe'—I opened my eyes. Instead of the approaching spears, I saw every spear lowered and many of the tribesmen moved to tears."

Reader 2:   Mr. Scott spent the remaining years of his life ministering Christ's love through word and song to his one-time adversaries.

Reader 1:   Though Edward Perronet wrote many other hymn texts, "All Hail the Power of Jesus' Name" is his only work to survive. How thankful we should be that God used this 18th century pastor to pen an inspiring text and then supplied the wings of melody to empower its use by worshiping believers around the world.

Reader 2:   May this timeless hymn of the church cause each of us to realize more fully what it means to truly worship our Lord even now and to prepare for the new song of praise that will continue throughout eternity with those from "every kindred and every tribe"—when together we "CROWN HIM LORD OF ALL."

*(Congregation sings "All Hail the Power of Jesus' Name,"
using the "[to be selected]" tune)*

See page 122, *101 Hymn Stories*

Drama 3

Amazing Grace

3 Characters: 2 Readers, John Newton

(Instruments begin by playing one stanza of "Amazing Grace")

Reader 1:   This familiar hymn is from the pen of a remarkable and colorful minister of the gospel, John Newton. Before his conversion he was known as a vile blasphemer and infidel—engaged in the despicable business of buying and then transporting black human beings as slaves to wealthy patrons around the world. On his tombstone in a small parish churchyard in Olney, England, can still be seen this inscription written by Newton himself:

Reader 2:   "John Newton, clerk, once an infidel and libertine, a servant of slavers in Africa, was, by the rich mercy of our Lord and Savior Jesus Christ, preserved, restored, pardoned, and appointed to preach the faith he had long labored to destroy."

Reader 1:   Until the time of his death at the age of 82, John Newton never ceased to marvel at the grace of God that had so dramatically transformed his sinful life. This was always the dominant theme of his preaching and writing.

Reader 2:   Shortly before Newton's death in 1807, a spokesman for the church suggested that the old pastor consider retirement because of his failing health, eyesight and memory. Newton responded—

John Newton: "What, shall the old African blasphemer stop while he can still speak?"

Reader 2:   On another occasion, just before his death, he is quoted as proclaiming from his pulpit with a loud voice—

John Newton: "My memory may be failing, but I will always remember two things: That I am a great sinner, and that Christ is a great Savior!"

Reader 2:   During these later years it was necessary for an assistant to stand in the pulpit to help Newton deliver his sermons. One Sunday he had repeated the words,

"Jesus Christ is precious." "You have already said that twice," whispered his helper; "go on."

John Newton: "I said that twice, and I am going to say it again."

Reader 2: Then the rafters rang as the old preacher shouted anew—

John Newton: "JESUS CHRIST IS PRECIOUS!"

Reader 1: John Newton's mother, a godly woman, died when he was just seven years of age. After several unhappy years of formal schooling at a boarding school, John left the school and joined his father's ship at the age of eleven to begin life as a seaman. His early years were one continuous round of rebellion and debauchery. After serving on several ships, Newton eventually became the captain of his own slave ship. Needless to say, the buying and selling and transporting of black slaves was a cruel and vicious way of life.

Reader 2: In 1748, while Newton was returning to England from Africa during a particularly stormy voyage that lasted nearly a month, it often appeared that all would be lost. Fearfully Newton began reading a book by Thomas à Kempis (Ah-KEM-pis) titled *The Imitation of Christ.* Thomas was a Dutch monk who lived during the fifteenth century and belonged to a religious order called "The Brethren of the Common Life." This book and the Scriptures were used by the Holy Spirit to sow the seeds of John's conversion during the frightening experience at sea.

John Newton: "'Twas grace that taught my heart to fear, and grace my fears relieved; how precious did that grace appear the hour I first believed."

Reader 1: At the age of 39, John Newton was ordained by the state church of England and began his first pastorate at the parish church in Olney, a small community of poor farmers and lacemakers.

Reader 2: Especially effective during this Olney ministry was the often related story of his early life and conversion experience. In addition to preaching for the stated services in his own church, Newton would hold meetings in any large building that could be secured in the surrounding area. This was an unheard-of practice for an Anglican clergyman of that day. But wherever he preached, large crowds gathered to hear the "old converted slave trader and sea captain."

Reader 1:   Another of Newton's unusual practices at the Olney Church was the singing of hymns that expressed the simple, heartfelt truths of his preaching rather than using only the stately psalms from the Psalter.

Reader 2:   When Newton couldn't find enough appropriate hymns for his purpose he began writing his own. He also enlisted the help of his friend and neighbor, William Cowper (KOO-per), a well-known author of classic literature. In 1779 their combined efforts produced the *Olney Hymns Hymnal*, one of the important contributions made to evangelical hymnody. "Amazing Grace" was one of the nearly 300 hymns written by John Newton for that collection.

Reader 1:   The tune for this text is an early American folk melody—a plantation song titled "Loving Lambs." It was first published with John Newton's "Amazing Grace" text in 1831, nearly 25 years after his death. During the remainder of the nineteenth century there was scarcely a hymnal published throughout our country that did not include this hymn.

(Instruments begin playing softly)

✻ ✻ ✻ ✻

Reader 2:   And still today, "Amazing Grace," with its simply stated text and singable folk melody, is one of the favorite hymns of God's people everywhere. We as believers should never lose the appreciation of God's gift of grace—providing our eternal salvation, meeting our daily needs, and guiding us to our heavenly home.

John Newton: "AMAZING GRACE, THAT SAVED A WRETCH LIKE ME!"

✻ ✻ ✻ ✻

(Congregation sings "Amazing Grace")

See page 28, *101 Hymn Stories*

America, the Beautiful

3 Characters: 2 Readers, Katharine Bates

(Instruments begin by playing a portion of "America, the Beautiful")

Reader 1: "To have put the expression of the highest and deepest patriotism into the mouths of a hundred million Americans is a monument so noble and so enduring that it seems as if no poet could possibly ask or expect anything more complete."

Reader 2: This tribute was given in a memorial service for Katharine Lee Bates at the time of her death in 1929. Her poem—AMERICA, THE BEAUTIFUL—had already become one of our country's favorite patriotic hymns.

Reader 1: Katharine Bates was born in Falmouth, Massachusetts, in 1859. Katharine gave nearly half a century of her life to Wellesley (WELLS-ly) College. She arrived there as a seventeen-year-old student and died there as a professor of English literature at the age of seventy. She became widely acclaimed as a literary specialist and was honored with doctorate degrees from several universities.

Reader 2: "America, the Beautiful" was never intended to become a hymn text. Katharine's first desire was to write a poem commemorating the four hundredth anniversary of Columbus' discovery of America. The following year, while visiting and teaching during the summer months in the state of Colorado, she received further inspiration for her patriotic lines.

Reader 1: It was while viewing the countryside from the beautiful summit of Pike's Peak, a mountain which towers more than 14,000 feet above sea level, that the desire to write a text describing the majesty and vastness of our great land prompted the poetic talents of Miss Bates.

Katharine Bates: "As I was looking out over the sea-like expanse of fertile country spreading away so far under the ample skies, the opening lines of this text formed themselves in my mind."

Reader 1: Later Miss Bates visited the Columbian Exposition of the World's Fair in Chicago where magnificent buildings were erected. Every structure was a masterpiece of planning, construction, and beauty. Thousands of people came from all over the world to marvel at the splendor of such a spectacle. Katharine, too, was deeply moved—

Katharine Bates: "The expression 'Alabaster Cities' was the direct result of my visit to Chicago in 1893. It made such a strong appeal to my patriotic feelings that it was in no small degree responsible for at least the last stanza. It was my desire to compare the unusual beauties of God's nature with the distinctive spectacles created by man."

Reader 2: This entire text sparkles with vivid, descriptive language. It reminds us so forcibly of our nation's heritage—the founding Pilgrims and the liberating heroes and patriots. Then each stanza is rounded off with the earnest prayer that God will always help our land attain its real destiny.

Katharine Bates: "Unless we crown our good with brotherhood, of what lasting value will be our spacious skies, our amber waves of grain, our majestic mountains, or our fruited plains? We must match the greatness of our country with the goodness of personal godly living."

Reader 1: The tune for this hymn is known as "Materna," a word which means "motherly." Composed by a New Jersey business man, Samuel Ward, it was originally intended for a different hymn text, "O Mother Dear, Jerusalem." Miss Bates was never completely happy with this tune, however, and always desired that new music might some day be composed especially for her text.

Reader 2: The hymn attained widespread popularity for the first time during the difficult days of World War I, when it did much to encourage patriotic pride and loyalty among the American people.

Reader 1: "America, the Beautiful" enjoys the distinction of being the first song ever used in outer space. In 1960, as our communications satellite Echo One orbited high above the earth, it received and relayed to the United States this hymn.

Reader 2: Before her death in 1929, Miss Bates commented about her hymn's growing popularity:

Katharine Bates: "That this hymn has gained in less than twenty years such a hold upon our people is clearly due to the fact that Americans are at heart idealists, with a fundamental faith in human brotherhood."

(Instruments begin playing softly)

✻ ✻ ✻ ✻

Reader 1: As we reflect on our nation's history during this particular season, may these words by Katharine Bates also be our earnest prayer for the future of our land—

Katharine Bates: "America! America! May God thy gold refine, till all success be nobleness, and every gain divine."

✻ ✻ ✻ ✻

(Congregation sings "America, the Beautiful")

See page 34, *101 More Hymn Stories*

- "After what I owe to God, nothing should be more dear or more sacred than the love and respect I owe to my country."   —Jacques Auguste de Thou

- "Active citizens of the heavenly kingdom must not be passive citizens of their earthly kingdom."
                                    —Author unknown

- "To be born free is a great privilege. To die free is an awesome responsibility."   —Author unknown

Drama 5

Battle Hymn of the Republic

3 Characters: 2 Readers, Julia Ward Howe

Reader 1:   Music has a unique way of arousing strong feelings of patriotism. Today's hymn has been unrivaled for inspiring these noble responses whenever this music is heard—

(Instruments play a portion of "Battle Hymn of the Republic")

Reader 1:   This familiar patriotic hymn, "The Battle Hymn of the Republic," was written by Julia Ward Howe during the early years of the Civil War.

Reader 2:   Deeply anguished at the growing conflict between the two sections of the country, Mrs. Howe often watched troops marching off to combat singing "John Brown's Body," a song about a man who had been hanged in his efforts to free the slaves. Julia felt strongly that this catchy camp meeting tune should be sung with better words.

Reader 1:   One day, as a parade of soldiers passed by singing this song, a visiting friend turned to Mrs. Howe— "Julia, why don't you write some decent words for that tune?"

Julia Howe: "That I will!"

Reader 2:   The new words came to her that same night.

Julia Howe: "I awoke in the gray of the morning, and as I lay waiting for the dawn, the long lines of the desired poem began to entwine themselves in my mind, and I said to myself, 'I must get up and write these verses down, lest I fall asleep and forget them.' So I sprang out of bed and in the dimness found an old stump of a pen which I remembered using the day before. I scrawled the verses almost without looking at the paper."

Reader 1:   The text first appeared in the *Atlantic Monthly Magazine* in 1862 as a battle song for the republic. Soon, however, the entire nation was united in singing these new words—"Mine eyes have seen the glory of the

Reader 1: coming of the Lord . . ."—rather than the many derisive phrases in "John Brown's Body."

Reader 2: Mrs. Howe's text was destined for immortality. After more than a century, Americans throughout the entire land still join often in proclaiming, "Glory, Glory, Hallelujah! His truth is marching on!"

Reader 1: On one occasion at a large patriotic rally President Lincoln heard the hymn sung. As the audience responded with loud applause, the President, with tears in his eyes, cried out—

Reader 2: "SING IT AGAIN"—

Reader 1: And again it was sung with great enthusiasm.

Reader 2: The "Battle Hymn of the Republic" soon became accepted as one of our finest national hymns. It found its way into almost every American hymnal published, with its original purpose of serving as a battle song for the Northern Republic during the Civil War soon forgotten.

Reader 1: Julia Ward Howe was a remarkable woman. Many of her ancestors were famous in American Revolutionary history. At the age of 29, Julia married the well-known humanitarian, Dr. Samuel Gridley Howe, who later became director of the Perkins Institute for the Blind in Boston, Massachusetts.

Reader 2: After her marriage to Dr. Howe, Julia became actively involved in such noble pursuits as opposition to slavery and the Women's Suffrage Movement. Five years after the Civil War she organized an international crusade urging all women of the world to unite for the purpose of ending war for all time.

Reader 1: Julia Ward Howe continued working for causes of human rights until her death in Newport, Rhode Island, in 1910, at the age of 91. Just 12 days before her death, she was awarded an honorary Doctor of Laws degree from Smith College for her lifelong accomplishments.

Reader 2: Although the "Battle Hymn of the Republic" gave Mrs. Howe her first national acclaim, she was also known for other publications, including three volumes of poetry. In addition, this remarkable woman was the mother of four children, all of whom distinguished themselves in the fields of science and literature.

(Instruments begin playing softly)

* * * *

Reader 1:   In reflecting upon the history of our country, we feel certain that the blessings we have enjoyed for more than two centuries are a direct result of the spiritual foundations laid for us by our forefathers. These blessings will remain only as God's truth continues to march on—as we His people diligently exercise our Christian responsibility in today's society—ever witnessing to the truth that . . .

Reader 2:   "righteousness exalteth a nation, but sin is a reproach to any people" (Proverbs 14:34).

Together: "Blessed is the nation whose God is the Lord" (Psalm 33:12).

* * * *

(Congregation sings "Battle Hymn of the Republic")

See page 34, *101 Hymn Stories*

Because He Lives

4 Characters: 2 Readers, Bill Gaither, Gloria Gaither

Reader 1:   The message of the empty tomb is the very heart-beat of the Christian faith. The Scriptures state this truth clearly: *Believing that God has raised Christ from the dead is essential for experiencing the new birth* (Romans 10:9). And because Christ is now alive and seated at the Father's right hand, we have the assurance that we will live and reign with Him eternally.

Reader 2:   "Where, O death, is your victory? Where, O death, is your sting? The sting of death is sin, and the power of sin is the law. But thanks be to God! He gives us the victory through our Lord Jesus Christ" (1 Corinthians 15:55, 56).

(Instruments play the chorus of "Because He Lives")

Reader 1:   Our featured hymn for this service, "Because He Lives," has enjoyed widespread popularity since it was chosen as the gospel song of the year in 1974. It is one of the more than 500 songs written by Bill and Gloria Gaither during the past two decades. Other favorites include:

Reader 2:   "He Touched Me," "Something Beautiful," "Let's Just Praise the Lord," "The King Is Coming," "There's Something About That Name," and "I Am Loved."

Reader 1:   But highlighting the Gaithers' entire ministry and reflecting their personal philosophy is the conviction that a believer's spiritual strength for coping with the demands of daily living is possible only *Because He Lives!*

The circumstances that prompted this hymn's writing are recalled by Bill Gaither—

Bill Gaither: "We wrote 'Because He Lives' after a period of time when we had a kind of dry spell and hadn't written any new songs for awhile. Also at the end of the 1960's when our country was going through some great turmoil with the height of the drug culture and the whole 'God is Dead' movement, which was running wild, and also at the peak of the Vietnam War, our little son Benjy was born. I thought, 'Brother, this is really a poor time to bring a child into the world.' At times Gloria and I were really quite discouraged by the whole thing. We had two little girls whom we loved very much, but this was our first son. Soon this lyric came to us—"

Gloria Gaither: * "How sweet to hold a new-born baby and feel the pride and joy he gives; But greater still the calm assurance: This child can face uncertain days because Christ lives. Because He lives I can face tomorrow; because He lives all fear is gone; because I know He holds the future and life is worth the living—just because He lives."

Bill Gaither: "And it gave us the courage to say because Christ lives we can face tomorrow and keep our heads high, and hopefully that could be of meaning to other people as well."

Reader 2: The Gaithers are always pleased when they receive word that "Because He Lives" has been a spiritual encouragement and comfort to others.

Bill Gaither: "It's rather interesting now that, although we don't consider ourselves as old writers, we've had many people tell us they have used that song at a funeral of a loved one; and it has been very encouraging to them, at a time when they were very discouraged. So evidently a lot of people have shared the same kind of experience of being discouraged."

Reader 1: In 1959 Bill Gaither began teaching English and journalism in his home town of Alexandria, Indiana.

Reader 2: There he met Gloria Sickal, who taught French and English in the same high school. Soon they began singing "Gaither music" in churches throughout the area and were married in 1962.

Reader 1:   Shortly Gloria and Bill left the teaching profession to pursue a full-time ministry of writing, recording albums, and performing numerous live concerts each year.

Reader 2:   Gloria has written a number of popular books, including *Rainbows at Easter*, and has co-authored with her husband their many gospel songs and musicals as well as an excellent church hymnal titled *Hymns for the Family of God*. Bill explains the choice for this title—

Bill Gaither: "Gloria and I have had a real concern that Christians need not be ostracized because of differences in the way they worship. We are all part of the same family, and the hymnal tries to preserve the best from many theological traditions. Therefore the broad name of this hymnal seems to cover exactly what we are trying to do."

Reader 2:   Bill was asked what he desired from the Lord for their future.

Bill Gaither: "I hope we can always remain open to different new ways of preaching and singing the gospel. Hopefully, what we are doing is not only preparing people to spend eternity with the Lord, but even preparing them to enjoy it more fully with Him."

Reader 1:   The message of the empty tomb is truly the very cornerstone of Christian worship. Without it, Christianity would be merely another religious system based on the teachings of a dead leader. But these dynamic changes began with Christ's resurrection—

Reader 2:   With the resurrection came a new day for worship—the first day of the week rather than the traditional Sabbath. Every Sunday is really an Easter celebration of the new life that is ours because of Christ's victory over sin and the grave.

Reader 1:   With the resurrection came the thrilling pronouncement of our immortality—"BECAUSE I LIVE, YOU ALSO WILL LIVE!" (John 14:19).

(Instruments play softly during the prayer)

✳   ✳   ✳   ✳

Gloria Gaither: (Prayer) Heavenly Father, we rejoice as we remember the empty tomb. We are grateful for a risen, ascended Savior, who even now sits at Your right hand to intercede for us. Fill us, Lord, with the power and joy of the resurrection as we seek to live and serve for Your glory. May the truths of this hymn be the encouragement we need to live victoriously each day and to share this transforming message with others.

*   *   *   *

(Congregation sings "Because He Lives")

See page 46, *101 More Stories*

- "Christianity begins where religion ends—with the resurrection"   —Author unknown

- "Arise, O soul, this Easter Day!
  Forget the tomb of yesterday,
  For thou from bondage art set free;
  Thou sharest in His victory.
  And life eternal is for thee,
  Because the Lord is risen."

  —Author unknown

Beyond the Sunset

4 Characters: 2 Readers, Virgil P. Brock, Horace Burr

Reader 1:   In this day of the disposable and the temporary, Christians must live with an awareness of eternity. The apostle Paul reminded the believers at Corinth that if their hope in Christ was only related to this life, they would be the most miserable of men (1 Corinthians 15:19). The anticipation of God's tomorrow makes it possible for Christians to live victoriously and joyfully today regardless of life's circumstances.

Reader 2:   One of the best known and most widely used gospel hymns about heaven was written by Virgil P. Brock.

(Instruments begin playing "Beyond the Sunset" and continue softly behind the telling of the story)

* * * *

Virgil P. Brock: "'Beyond the Sunset' was born during a conversation at the dinner table one evening in 1936. We had been watching a very unusual sunset at Winona Lake, Indiana, with a blind guest—my cousin Horace Burr—and his wife Grace. A large area of the water appeared ablaze with the glory of God, yet there were threatening storm clouds gathering overhead. Returning to our home, we went to the dinner table still talking about the impressive spectacle we had witnessed. Our blind guest remarked:

Horace Burr: *(blind)*—"I have never seen a more beautiful sunset."

Virgil P. Brock: "But cousin Horace, people are always amazed when you talk about seeing, when they know that you have always been blind."

Horace Burr: "But I can see . . . for I see through other people's eyes; and I think I often see more clearly than they do—because I see beyond the sunset."

Virgil P. Brock: "It was that phrase, 'beyond the sunset,' and the striking inflection of his voice that struck me so forcibly . . . I began singing the first few measures. Then his wife interrupted me—'That's beautiful . . . Virgil; please go to the piano and sing that phrase again.' We went to the piano nearby and soon completed the first verse."

Horace Burr: "Virgil, now you should have a verse about the storm clouds."

Virgil P. Brock: "And the words for this verse came quickly as well. Recalling how closely our guests Horace and Grace had walked hand in hand together for so many years due to his blindness, the third verse was soon added. Before the evening meal was finished, all four stanzas had been written and we sang the entire song together with much excitement."

✳ ✳ ✳ ✳

Reader 1:   In his book of memoirs, written two years before his home-going in 1976 at the age of 91, Virgil Brock recalls numerous incidents from his active and colorful Christian life:

Virgil P. Brock: "I was born on January 6, 1887, in a rural community several miles southeast of Celina, Ohio. I was the sixth of eight sons born to my Quaker parents. My parents were devout and firm in their spiritual convictions. They abhorred liquor, tobacco, and corrupt speech, and ardently practiced what they believed to be the teaching of the Bible. I was converted at the age of 16, at a nearby church revival meeting. Soon I felt the call for Christian service and prepared myself with studies at the Fairmont Friends Academy and Earlham College in Indiana. During this time I pastored several small Quaker churches. Some time later, I met and married a talented singer and pianist named Blanche Kerr—'The Belle of the Community.'"

Reader 2:   Until Blanche's death from cancer in 1958, the Brocks were actively involved in evangelism and much song writing. In the Warsaw-Winona Lake cemetery, a large monument was erected for Blanche with the words and music of "Beyond the Sunset" fully engraved in stone as a tribute to the dedicated ministries of this talented couple. Most of the more than 500 gospel songs written by Virgil Brock were in collaboration with his wife Blanche.

(Instruments begin playing softly)

* * * *

Reader 1: But the one song for which the Christian church will be eternally grateful to Mr. and Mrs. Brock is this promise of hope for every child of God—the heavenly home that awaits believers beyond the storms and sunsets of this life.

Virgil P. Brock: "Beyond the sunset, O blissful morning . . . beyond the sunset—forevermore."

* * * *

(Congregation sings "Beyond the Sunset")

See page 48, *101 More Hymn Stories*

- "Heaven will be the endless portion of every man who has heaven in his soul" —Henry Ward Beecher

- "An eternal hope is the oxygen of the human soul."
  —Author unknown

Drama 8

Blest Be the Tie that Binds

8 Characters: 2 Readers, 4 village people, John Fawcett, Mary Fawcett

(Instruments begin playing one verse of this hymn)

Reader 1: One of the blessings of the Christian life is the fellowship we enjoy with other believers. It was an appreciation for the strong bond of love and concern between a pastor and his people that inspired this well-loved hymn.

Reader 2: John Fawcett was a young and obscure Baptist pastor in the bleak little village of Wainsgate, England, in the year 1782.

(Four poorly dressed people gather with baskets and bundles at the village meeting place.)

No. 1: Did you hear the dreadful news? Pastor Fawcett is leavin' us—and soon!

No. 2: No! But he can't! What'd we ever do without 'im? He's a great preacher . . . and we all love 'im so much . . . .

No. 3: He won't leave us, will he? Where's he goin'?

No. 1: He just had a call—to preach at that big Carter's Lane Baptist Church—away up in London. He's gonna take the place of that famous preacher, Dr. Gill.

No. 4: But doesn't he know how much we've always loved 'im and Mrs. Fawcett—ever since they arrived here just after their weddin'—with nothin' but their clothin' and a few books?

No. 2: He was only 26 years old when he come. But he was so kind and helpful! He soon won us over. We've all been devoted to 'im and 'is dear family ever since.

No. 1: And his preachin's been so inspirin' and helpful all these years. That's why those people in that big rich church in London have heard about 'im and want 'im.

No. 3: I've been 'fraid this might happen to us someday. Our poor little church up here in the hills just can't keep up with churches like Carter's Lane.

No. 2: But what'll we ever do here at Wainsgate when the Fawcett family leaves us? We just can't let 'em go!

No. 4:   Let's really pray hard that God'll keep our dear pastor and 'is family with us just a little longer.

Reader 1:   But moving day soon came. Pastor Fawcett's farewell sermon had been preached and the wagons were being loaded with the family's belongings. The parishioners were gathered around to say their tearful goodbyes.

John Fawcett: "There . . . that finishes it—books, furniture and all the trunks of clothing . . . I think we're finally ready to move on . . . God bless you all, my dear people; and may He give you very soon another leader who will be able to help you even more than we've tried to do these past seven years."

No. 2:   But Pastor Fawcett . . . you just can't leave us . . . please—we all love you and need you too much.

No. 3:   We're brokenhearted 'cause you're goin'. You've done so much for us—you've taught us most of all what it really means to love and trust God.

No. 1:   We've been prayin' for a week that God'll make you change your plans and stay with us.

*(A moment of silence as John and Mary Fawcett
look sorrowfully at each other)*

Mary Fawcett: "Oh, John, I cannot bear this. I do not know how we can leave this place and all these dear people. How can we break the tie of affection that binds our hearts to these dear friends?"

John Fawcett: *(hesitation)* "Mary, I feel as you do. I don't know how we can leave! *(pause . . . then with cheerful determination)* We shall remain here with our people. Let's unload those wagons and get on with our work. My dear friends, Mary and I have just changed our minds. We have decided to remain here at Wainsgate with you."

Everyone (talking at once):   Glory be to God . . . God bless our pastor and 'is family . . . Let God's name be ever praised for His blessings to us this day . . . .

John Fawcett: "Dear people, let this experience ever remind us of the truth of God's Word that the fellowship of kindred minds is like to that above. I feel that God would have me write my feelings this day in a poem for all of you. I will share these thoughts with you in one of my sermons very soon."

Reader 1:   The next Sunday with the farewell experience still vivid in his mind, Pastor Fawcett shared this text with his Wainsgate parishioners:

John Fawcett: "Blest be the tie that binds our hearts in Christian love; the fellowship of kindred minds is like to that above. Before our Father's throne we pour our ardent prayers; our fears, our hopes, our aims are one, our comforts and our cares. We share our mutual woes, our mutual burdens bear; and often for each other flows the sympathizing tear. When we asunder part, it gives us inward pain; but we shall still be joined in heart and hope to meet again. This glorious hope revives our courage for the way; when each in expectation lives and longs to see the day when from sorrow, toil, pain and sin, we shall be free; and perfect love and joy shall reign through all eternity."

Reader 1:   John Fawcett continued his faithful ministry to these humble people at Wainsgate until a paralytic stroke caused his death in 1817, at the age of 77. His salary was estimated at never more than $200.00 per year, in spite of his growing reputation as an outstanding evangelical preacher and scholar. In recognition of his ministry and many accomplishments, including the establishment of a school for the training of nonconformist men for the ministry, Brown University in America conferred the Doctor of Divinity degree upon him in 1811. On another occasion, the King of England is said to have offered John Fawcett any gift he might desire. His reply was . . .

John Fawcett: "I have the love of my people—I need nothing more that even a king could provide."

Reader 2:   John Fawcett's life is a model of a spiritual leader who sacrificed ambition and personal gain for Christian devotion to God and His people.

(Congregation sings "Blest Be the Tie That Binds")

See page 45, *101 Hymn Stories*

Come, Thou Fount of Every Blessing

4 Characters: 2 Readers, Robert Robinson, Lady Traveler

Reader 1: We are featuring today a praise song that many of us have known since we were children in Sunday school. Yet we never outgrow our enjoyment of this joyful expression of praise—

> *(Instruments play a portion of*
> *"Come, Thou Fount of Every Blessing")*

Reader 2: This familiar hymn, "Come, Thou Fount of Every Blessing," was written by Robert Robinson, a twenty-three-year-old English minister.

Reader 1: Robert Robinson was born of lowly parents in Norfolk, England, in 1735. The father died when his son was only eight, and at the age of fourteen young Robert was sent to London to learn the barbering trade. Here for the next three years he mixed with a notorious gang of hoodlums and lived a life of debauchery.

Reader 2: At the age of seventeen Robert and his gang attended a meeting where the noted evangelist George Whitefield (WHIT-field) was preaching.

Reader 1: Although he had intended to "scoff at those poor, deluded Methodists," young Robert was so impressed and convicted by Whitefield's strong evangelistic preaching that he soon professed faith in Christ as his Savior. Before long he felt called to enter the ministry.

Reader 2: Robinson first became pastor of a Methodist church and later served in a large Baptist church in Cambridge, England.

Reader 1: Despite his youth, Robert Robinson became known as an able minister and scholar. He wrote various theological books as well as several hymns.

   In singing "Come, Thou Fount," have you ever wondered about the interesting phrase found in the second stanza of this hymn? . . .

Reader 2:   "Here I raise mine Ebenezer, hither by Thy help I come."

Reader 1:   Often we sing words such as these without fully realizing what they mean. This particular line refers to the account in 1 Samuel 7 where the Ebenezer or stone was raised by Samuel as a symbolic memorial of God's faithfulness to His chosen people.

Reader 2:   "While Samuel was sacrificing the burnt offering, the Philistines drew near to engage Israel in battle. But that day the Lord thundered with loud thunder against the Philistines and threw them into such a panic that they were routed before the Israelites. The men of Israel rushed out of Mizpah and pursued the Philistines, slaughtering them along the way . . . Then Samuel took a stone and set it up and named it Ebenezer, saying, 'Thus far has the Lord helped us.' So the Philistines were subdued and did not invade Israelite territory again" (1 Samuel 7:10-13).

Reader 1:   Another interesting expression in the third stanza of this hymn is, "Prone to wander, Lord, I feel it— prone to leave the God I love."

Reader 2:   Although Robinson wrote these lines as a young man, it was prophetic of his later years. After nearly a lifetime of ministering the gospel to others, Robinson lapsed into sin and doubt and began to follow the doctrines of Unitarianism.

Reader 1:   One day as Robinson was traveling in a stagecoach through England, he noticed a lady passenger across from him deeply engrossed in her hymnbook.

Robert Robinson: "Excuse me, Madam, but could that be a hymnbook you are reading?"

Lady Traveler: "Oh, my good man, I have just discovered the most delightful hymn in my hymnal. Let me read to you several of its lines:

'Come, Thou fount of ev'ry blessing, tune my heart to sing Thy grace;
Streams of mercy, never ceasing, call for songs of loudest praise.
Teach me some melodious sonnet sung by flaming tongues above.

Praise the mount—I'm fixed upon it—mount of Thy
redeeming love.'"

Robert Robinson: "O Madam, thank you for reading those
words for me. I am the poor unhappy soul who wrote
that text many years ago, and I would give a thousand
worlds, if I had them, to enjoy the same feelings I knew
then."

Reader 1:   One of the hazards of growing older is that many
tend to lose the joy and spiritual vitality they once enjoyed. Instead of fulfilling the scriptural directive of singing "with the Spirit and with understanding" (1
Corinthians 14:15), now they merely mumble along
weakly during times of congregational praise. Let us
pause and breathe out this prayer of personal renewal
to our God—

Reader 2:   "Restore unto me the *joy* of Thy salvation . . . open
Thou my lips, and my mouth shall show forth Thy
praise" (Psalm 51:12, 15 KJV).

Reader 1:   And the writer of the Book of Hebrews further
reminds us that we are to offer the sacrifice of praise to
God continually—to give thanks to His name . . . "for
with such sacrifices God is pleased" (Hebrews 13:15).

(Instruments begin playing softly)

* * * *

Reader 2:   May the singing of this hymn as well as the tragic
example of its author remind us of the importance of
maintaining a lifelong "sacrifice of praise." Let us deter-
mine to say with the psalmist David—

Together: I WILL PRAISE THE LORD ALL MY LIFE: I WILL SING PRAISE TO
GOD AS LONG AS I LIVE" (Psalm 146:2).

* * * *

(Congregation sings "Come, Thou Fount of Every Blessing")

See page 51, *101 Hymn Stories*

Day by Day

4 Characters: 2 Readers, Lina Sandell, Oscar Ahnfelt

Reader 1: The victorious Christian life has been described as simply a fresh awareness of Christ's provisions of joy and power for each new day. Today's featured hymn was written by a young Swedish woman who learned early in life the important lesson of living daily with the conscious presence and renewing provisions of her Lord.

(Instruments play a portion of "Day by Day")

Reader 1: "Day by Day and with each passing moment . . . ," was written by the Swedish poetess, Lina Sandell, (San-DELL) who was called the "Fanny Crosby of Sweden" for her many contributions to gospel hymnody.

Reader 2: From the pen of Lina Sandell flowed a great number of hymns which contributed much to the waves of revival that were sweeping the Scandinavian countries during the latter half of the nineteenth century.

Reader 1: Lina was born in 1832 in a small community in northern Sweden where her father, Jonas Sandell, was the Lutheran parish pastor.

Reader 2: Though serving a state church, Pastor Sandell was sympathetic and strongly supportive of the revival movement. He became an early leader in this spiritual renewal with its emphasis on a personal salvation experience as opposed to reliance upon the sacraments and rituals of the church.

Reader 1: Lina greatly loved and admired her father. Since she was a frail youngster, she generally preferred to be with him in his study rather than with comrades outdoors.

Reader 2: When Lina was just twelve years of age, she had an experience that greatly shaped her entire life. At an early age she had been stricken with a partial paralysis that confined her to bed much of the time. Though the physicians considered her chance for a complete recovery hopeless, her parents always believed that God would in time make her well again.

Reader 1:   One Sunday morning while her parents were in church, Lina began reading the Bible and praying earnestly. When her parents returned, they were amazed to find her dressed and walking freely. After this experience of physical healing, Lina began to write verses expressing her gratitude and love for God and published her first book of spiritual poetry when she was sixteen.

Reader 2:   Some years later Lina was accompanying her father aboard ship across Lake Vattern (VAT-tern). As they stood on deck watching the rolling waves, the vessel suddenly lurched. Lina's father fell overboard and drowned before the eyes of his devoted daughter.

Reader 1:   Although Lina had written many hymn texts prior to this tragic experience, now more than ever poetic thoughts began to flow from her broken heart. All of her hymns reflect a tender, childlike trust in her Savior and a deep sense of His abiding presence in her life.

Reader 2:   Another familiar Swedish hymn from the pen of Lina Sandell is "Children of the Heavenly Father." In these lines she expressed the same complete confidence in God that her hymn "Day by Day" reveals.

(Instruments play softly "Children of the Heavenly Father" while words are read)

❋   ❋   ❋   ❋

Lina Sandell: "Children of the heav'nly Father safely in His bosom gather;
Nestling bird nor star in heaven such a refuge e'er was given.

God His own doth tend and nourish, in His holy courts they flourish;
From all evil things He spares them, in His mighty arms He bears them.

Though He giveth or He taketh, God His children ne'er
forsaketh;
His the loving purpose solely to preserve them pure
and holy."

* * * *

Reader 1: Lina Sandell wrote approximately 650 hymns before her death in 1903 at the age of 71. Fifty years after
her death, 10,000 people gathered in the yard of her
childhood home to dedicate a bronze statue in her memory. The little family cottage is now a public museum in
Sweden.

Reader 2: The remarkable popularity attained by Lina Sandell's hymns has been due partially to the simple but
melodious music written for them by Scandinavian musicians such as Oscar Ahnfelt, the composer of "Day by
Day." Ahnfelt was known as "the spiritual troubadour
of Scandinavia" in his day. Not only did he possess the
gift of composing pleasing melodies that caught the
fancy of the Swedish people, but he traveled from village to village throughout the Scandinavian countries
preaching and singing these folklike hymns to the accompaniment of his home-made ten string guitar. Lina
Sandell once said of him—

Lina Sandell: "Ahnfelt has sung my songs into the hearts of
the people."

Reader 1: As is often true whenever revival fires begin to
glow, Oscar Ahnfelt experienced much opposition. One
time King Karl the 15th was petitioned to forbid Ahnfelt's ministry throughout the Scandinavian countries.
When the monarch called for him to appear at the court,
Ahnfelt could not decide what he should sing for his
king, so he requested Lina Sandell to write a special
poem for the occasion. Within a few days she had the
new text ready. With his guitar under his arm and the
new hymn in his pocket, Ahnfelt appeared at the royal
palace and sang these tender words—

Oscar Ahnfelt: "Who is it that knocketh upon your heart's
door in peaceful eve?

Who is it that brings to the wounded and sore the balm
that can heal and relieve?
Your heart is still restless; it findeth no peace in earth's
pleasures;
Your heart is still yearning; it seeketh release to
heavenly treasures."

Reader 1:   King Karl listened with moist eyes. When Ahnfelt
had finished, the monarch gripped him by the hand
and exclaimed . . .

Reader 2:   "You may sing and preach as much as you desire
throughout all of my kingdom."

(Instruments begin playing softly)

* * * *

Reader 1:   How thankful we should be that as believers in
Christ we can enjoy an intimate relationship with the
God of the universe. May the reassuring words of Lina
Sandell's hymns as well as the faithful promises from
God's Word itself be our source of encouragement as
we face the unknowns of each new day—

Reader 2:   "As thy days, so shall thy strength be" (Deuterono-
my 33:25 KJV). "Be strong and courageous. Do not be
terrified; do not be discouraged, for the Lord your God
will be with you wherever you go" (Joshua 1:9).

Together: "MY GRACE IS SUFFICIENT FOR YOU!" (2 Corinthians 12:9).

* * * *

*(Congregation sings "Day by Day" and possibly
"Children of the Heavenly Father")*

See page 57, *101 Hymn Stories*

Drama 11

Deeper and Deeper

3 Characters: 2 Readers, Oswald Smith

(Instruments begin by playing a portion of "Deeper and Deeper")

Reader 1: Our featured hymn for this service, "Deeper and Deeper," expresses the yearnings of one of the truly outstanding evangelical pastors, evangelists and missionary statesmen of the twentieth century—Oswald J. Smith.

Reader 2: For many years the name of Dr. Smith has been recognized as the founder in 1928 of the well-known People's Church of Toronto, Canada. This congregation has since become widely acclaimed for its generous support of world-wide missions.

Reader 1: The oldest of ten children, Oswald Smith was born in 1889, in a secluded farm house on the outskirts of Odessa, Ontario, Canada. He accepted Christ as his personal Savior in the city of Toronto at a large evangelistic campaign conducted by evangelist R.A. Torrey.

Oswald Smith: "Then suddenly it happened. I cannot explain it even today. I just bowed my head, put my face between my hands and in a moment the tears gushed through my fingers and fell on the chair, and there stole into my boyish heart a realization of the fact that the great change had taken place. Christ had entered my life and I was a new creature. I had been born again. There was no excitement, no unusual feeling, but I knew that something had happened, and ever after, all of life would be different. That was on January 28, 1906, when I was sixteen years of age, and it has lasted to this day. Yes, and it is going to last, praise God, throughout the countless ages of eternity!"

Reader 2: About two years after this conversion experience, Oswald Smith felt the call of God to preach the gospel. He attended evening classes for a time at the Toronto Bible College and soon was out preaching in missions, prisons, youth groups—wherever he could find listeners to the good news of salvation. Dr. Smith often looked back on his long lifetime in the Christian ministry.

Oswald Smith: "If I could go back to 1906, after having experienced the ups and downs of the Christian life, I would do again exactly what I did then; I would open my heart to the Lord Jesus and accept Him as my personal Savior. And if I could go back to 1908 when I first began to preach—after having known the ups and downs of a minister's life—I would once again decide for the ministry of the Lord Jesus Christ: I would give my life once more to the greatest work in the world—the proclamation of the gospel!"

Reader 1:   After graduation from McCormick Theological Seminary in Chicago and after he had served as pastor of several churches in Canada and in the United States, Dr. Smith founded the People's Church in 1928.

Oswald Smith: "Why should anyone hear the gospel twice before everyone has heard it once . . . ?"

Reader 1:   Was a challenging statement often heard as Dr. Smith ministered from this pulpit as well as at missionary conferences around the world.

Reader 2:   Dr. Smith authored 35 books, which have been translated into more than 100 languages. He has also written approximately 1,200 hymns, poems and gospel songs.

Reader 1:   His familiar hymn "Deeper and Deeper" was composed in this way:

Oswald Smith: "I was traveling secretary of the Pocket Testament League, founded by Mrs. Charles Alexander. Arriving in Woodstock, Ontario, one day in the year 1911, I was invited to preach one Sunday morning in the largest Methodist Church in that city. As I walked along the street on my way to the church, the melody of this hymn suddenly sang itself into my heart and with it these words—

(Recite or sing the words—"Into the heart of Jesus,
Deeper and Deeper I Go")

I can still recall the joy and buoyancy of youth, the bright sunshine overhead, and the thrill with which I looked forward to my service that Sunday morning, as again and again I hummed over the words. I wondered if I could retain the music in my mind until the service was over. I was just 21 years of age. After preaching, I quickly returned to my rented room and the first thing I did was to write out the melody as God had given it to me. I had been able to remember it, and it has never changed from that day to this."

Reader 2:   The writing of the remaining verses was much more difficult. Three years later, however, while pastoring the First Presbyterian Church of South Chicago, Dr. Smith completed his hymn.

Oswald Smith: "It was then 1914, and I was 24 years old. The writing of the hymn afforded me much joy, nor has it ever grown old. I still love it and always will, for it was the child of my youth. It proves conclusively that God can impart His deepest truths to the hearts of the young, for I doubt I have ever written anything more profound since."

(Instruments begin playing softly)

✳ ✳ ✳ ✳

Reader 1:   In 1986, at the age of 96, Dr. Oswald J. Smith completed his life's work and realized the full meaning of these words written in the early years of his ministry—

Oswald Smith: "And through eternal ages, gratefully I shall sing—O how He loved—Jesus, my Lord and my King!"

✳ ✳ ✳ ✳

(Congregation sings "Deeper and Deeper")

See page 63, *101 Hymn Stories*

Doxology

3 Characters: 3 Readers

Reader 1: If asked what song has been sung more often in church services than any other, we would likely agree on this familiar music—

(Instruments play a portion of the "Doxology")

Reader 1: The Doxology—"Praise God from Whom All Blessings Flow"—has been sung more frequently than any other known song for more than 300 years. Nearly every English-speaking Protestant congregation unites at least once each Sunday in this noble ascription of praise.

Reader 2: The word "doxology" is taken from the Greek language and means an "offering of praise to God." There are several inspiring biblical doxologies; one is recorded in Jude 25—

Reader 3: "To the only God our Savior be glory, majesty, power and authority, through Jesus Christ our Lord, before all ages, now and forevermore! Amen."

Reader 1: Thomas Ken, the author of our musical doxology, was a bold, outspoken seventeenth century Anglican bishop who was born in England in the year 1637. Ken's illustrious career in the State Church of England was stormy and colorful. Following ordination in 1662, he served as chaplain to the Bishop of Winchester. Several years later he was sent to Holland, where he was the English chaplain at the royal court of the Hague (Haig).

Reader 2: But Chaplain Ken denounced so boldly the corrupt lives of those in authority in the Dutch capital that he was compelled to leave after just one year. Upon his return to England, Ken was appointed to be the personal chaplain of King Charles II.

Reader 1: Chaplain Ken continued the same spirit of boldness in rebuking the sins of this pleasure-loving English monarch. Yet in spite of this practice, the king always admired his courageous, outspoken chaplain. He referred to him as the "good little man" and when it was chapel time King Charles would say—

Reader 3: "Now I must go in and hear Ken tell me my faults."

Reader 1: Soon the King rewarded Thomas Ken by appointing him to be the Anglican bishop of the prestigious Bath (Bahth) and Wells area. But just twelve days after Thomas Ken was consecrated as a bishop, Charles II died and was succeeded by his Catholic brother, James II. Before long Bishop Ken angered the new monarch and was imprisoned in the infamous Tower of London.

Reader 2: Although Ken was eventually acquitted, he was removed from his high office of bishop and forced to spend the remaining years of his life in obscurity until his death at the age of 74.

A noted historian has paid this tribute to the little bishop—

Reader 3: "He came as near to the ideal of Christian perfection as human weakness permits."

Reader 1: During his early ministry, Thomas Ken wrote a book titled *A Manual of Prayers for the Use of Scholars at Winchester College*. In this manual, Ken included three of his own hymns that he wished to have the students sing each day as part of their personal devotions. These were titled "Morning Hymn," "Evening Hymn," and "Midnight Hymn."

Reader 2: Each of these three hymns closed with the familiar four lines we now know as the Doxology.

Reader 3: "Praise God from whom all blessings flow . . ."

Reader 1: Each time we sing this phrase we acknowledge that God is the giver of every good and perfect gift.

Reader 3: "Praise Him all creatures here below . . ."

Reader 2: Here all of God's earthly creatures are exhorted to lift voices of praise to their Creator.

Reader 3: "Praise Him above ye heavenly host . . ."

Reader 1: Here praise is expanded to include the hosts of angelic choirs which surround the throne of God.

Reader 3: "Praise Father, Son and Holy Ghost."

Reader 2: This phrase reaffirms our belief in a Triune Godhead. It has been said that the singing of the Doxology does more to teach the doctrine of the Trinity than all of the theological books ever written.

Reader 3:   "There are three that bear record in heaven, the Father, the Word, and the Holy Spirit; and these three are one" (1 John 5:7 KJV).

(Instruments begin playing softly)

✳ ✳ ✳ ✳

Reader 1:   One of the important lessons for victorious Christian living is learning to translate our theology into a daily doxology. Often, however, we sing and use the same expressions so routinely in our personal devotions as well as in our church services that our worship of God tends to become a lifeless formality.

Reader 2:   As we sing the Doxology once again let us rededicate ourselves to the goal of offering praise to our God that is truly worthy of Him. May we recover our first love of worship and then join with the psalmist David in saying . . .

Reader 3:   "I will praise You, O Lord my God, with all my heart; I will glorify Your name forever" (Psalm 86:12).

✳ ✳ ✳ ✳

(Congregation stands and sings the "Doxology")

See page 66, *101 Hymn Stories*

Great Is Thy Faithfulness

3 Characters: 2 Readers, Thomas Chisholm

Reader 1: "Because of the Lord's great love we are not con-
sumed, for His compassions never fail. They are new
every morning; great is Your faithfulness" (Lamenta-
tions 3:22, 23).

Reader 2: One of the important lessons that the children of
Israel had to learn during their wilderness journey was
that God's provision of manna for them was on a morning-by-morning basis. They could not survive on old
manna nor could they store it for future use (Exodus
16:19-21).

(Instruments play a portion of "Great Is Thy Faithfulness")

Reader 1: Of the many gospel hymns written in recent times on
the theme of God's goodness and faithfulness, the hymn
"Great Is Thy Faithfulness" stands out like a beacon light.

Reader 2: While many hymns are born out of a particular
dramatic experience, this hymn was simply the result
of the author's "morning-by-morning" realization of
God's personal faithfulness in his life.

Reader 1: Thomas O. Chisholm (CHIS-olm) was born in a
crude log cabin in Franklin, Kentucky, in 1866.

Reader 2: From this humble beginning and without the benefit
of high school or advanced education, Thomas Chisholm
somehow began his career as a school teacher at the
age of sixteen in the same country school where he had
received his elementary education. After accepting Christ
as Savior, he became editor of the *Pentecostal Herald*.
Later he was ordained as a Methodist minister but was
soon forced to resign because of poor health. He began
working as an insurance agent and continued this until
he was 87 years old. Then he spent the remaining years
of his life at the Methodist Home for the Aged in Ocean
Grove, New Jersey. Shortly before his death at the age
of 94, Mr. Chisholm wrote—

Thomas Chisholm: "My income has never been large at any time due to impaired health in the earlier years which has followed me on until now. But I must not fail to record here the unfailing faithfulness of a covenant-keeping God and that He has given me many wonderful displays of His providing care which have filled me with astonishing gratefulness."

Reader 1:   In 1923, Mr. Chisholm sent this text and several of his other poems to W.M. Runyan, a prominent gospel musician and teacher associated with the Moody Bible Institute and an editor at the Hope Publishing Company.

Reader 2:   Mr. Runyan was so enthusiastic about "Great Is Thy Faithfulness" that he promptly composed appropriate music for it. He explained: "This particular poem held such an appeal to me that I prayed most earnestly that my tune might carry its message in a worthy way; and the subsequent history of its use indicates that God answered my prayer."

*(Instruments play the hymn softly and
continue to the close of the reading)*

✳   ✳   ✳   ✳

Reader 1:   What is it about a hymn such as this that ministers so effectively to us as Christians? Perhaps it is because whenever we have taken time to review the pleasant as well as the difficult experiences that have occurred in our lives, we simply must respond with overwhelming gratitude—"Great is Thy faithfulness, Lord, unto me."

Reader 2:   "Good when He gives, supremely good—nor less when He denies. Even crosses from His sovereign hand are blessings in disguise."   —Author unknown

Reader 1:   Or perhaps when we enjoy the sights of nature during the changing seasons of the year, once again we are awed by God's majesty. We realize anew that all nature gives "manifold witness to His great faithfulness, mercy and love."

Reader 2:   "His hand pours beauty from a shining cup upon green hills and leafy mountain ways;

That I may pause in wonder—looking up—and worship Him through all my length of days."

—Author unknown

Reader 1: Then I must rejoice greatly because this Creator-redeemer God is my personal Savior, my Friend, my Guide throughout this life and for all eternity—"Blessings all mine with ten thousand beside."

Reader 2: "How wonderful to walk with Thee! How wonderful to know

The hand once pierced on Calvary doth guide me as I go!"

—Author unknown

Reader 1: And from the second epistle of Timothy we learn this thrilling truth: "If we died with Him . . .

Reader 2: We will also live with Him;

Reader 1: If we endure . . .

Reader 2: We will also reign with Him.

Reader 1: And even if we are faithless,

Reader 2: HE WILL REMAIN FAITHFUL, FOR HE CANNOT DISOWN HIMSELF" (2 Timothy 2:11-13).

Reader 1: With Thomas Chisholm may we respond to God's "morning-by-morning faithfulness" with these words of praise . . .

Thomas Chisholm: "All I have needed Thy hand hath provided—Great is Thy faithfulness, Lord, unto me."

✳   ✳   ✳   ✳

(Congregation sings "Great Is Thy Faithfulness")

See page 83, *101 Hymn Stories*

He Hideth My Soul

4 Characters: 2 Readers, Fanny Crosby, William Kirkpatrick

Reader 1: A hymn writer well known to Christians everywhere is Fanny Crosby. She has written more hymns and supplied our church hymnal with more favorites than any other writer. At least 8,000 gospel texts flowed from the soul of this godly woman. Some of her best loved hymns are—

Reader 2: "Blessed Assurance," "Tell Me the Story of Jesus," "Rescue the Perishing," "To God Be the Glory," "Saved by Grace," and "All the Way My Savior Leads Me."

Reader 1: The story of Fanny Crosby's life as she triumphed over the handicap of blindness is most inspiring—

Fanny Crosby: "I was born of humble parents at Southeast, New York, in 1823. I was blinded for life through improper medical treatment when I was only six weeks of age. But I never considered blindness a handicap—rather a blessing and always insisted that blind people can accomplish almost everything that sighted persons can. I lived a normal, happy childhood. People often marveled that I could climb a tree like a squirrel and even ride a horse bareback. I began composing poetry when just a mere child. In fact, I recall writing these lines when I was only eight years of age—

Oh, what a happy soul am I;
Although I cannot see,
I am resolved that in this world
Contented I will be.

How many blessings I enjoy
That other people don't;
To weep and sigh because I'm blind,
I cannot, and I won't."

Reader 2:   Fanny Crosby continued writing poems, but they were always of a secular nature.

Fanny Crosby: "Once I wrote the text for a very popular song titled 'Rosalie, the Prairie Flower.' I can still recall the thrill of receiving a check for $3,000.00 for this little work."

Reader 2:   But one day William Bradbury, a friend who was well known as a gospel musician, confronted her with the challenge—"Fanny, don't you think it's time that you begin writing texts about the Lord—the One you profess to love so well?"

Fanny Crosby: "These words by William Bradbury began to bother me greatly. I had been a Christian for many years and a faithful member of the St. John's Methodist Episcopal Church of New York City. But I was already well into my forties, and the thought of writing religious verse seemed quite frightening. Yet, you know, spiritual thoughts and words began to flow freely from my heart and soon I was the happiest creature in all the land. Our home became a virtual beehive of activity as my many musician and pastor friends were always dropping in on me and requesting a new text for some special occasion. I can recall the day William Kirkpatrick stopped to see me in our New York home. He and I had worked together on numerous songs in the past."

William Kirkpatrick: "Fanny, I've just finished composing a new tune that I thought would make a singable hymn. May I play it for you on the piano?"

(Piano plays the first phrase of "He Hideth My Soul")

William Kirkpatrick: "Now I need some words that would make this tune communicate the idea of confidence— the confidence we can have in God as we place our complete trust in Him."

(Fanny closes her eyes in prayer as she grasps her Bible. Then her face lights up as these words begin to flow from her heart . . .)

Fanny Crosby: "A wonderful Savior is Jesus my Lord, a wonderful Savior to me;

He hideth my soul in the cleft of the rock, where rivers
of pleasure I see . . ."

Reader 1:   Fanny Jane Crosby lived to be 95 years of age. In
her later years, she was in much demand as a speaker
and lecturer throughout the entire country. She usually
traveled alone for these engagements and was often
introduced with such titles as "the Protestant Saint"
and "the most wonderful person living." It was her
continual prayer that God would allow her to be used
in leading to Christ every individual she contacted. Only
eternity will disclose the host of people who have been
won to a saving faith in her Lord or the number of lives
that have been spiritually enriched through her many
hymns.

(Instruments begin playing softly)

✳   ✳   ✳   ✳

Reader 2:   Engraved on Fanny Crosby's tombstone at Bridge-
port, Connecticut, are these significant words taken from
our Lord's remarks to Mary after she had anointed Him
with costly perfume—SHE HATH DONE WHAT SHE COULD
(Mark 14:8).

✳   ✳   ✳   ✳

(Congregation sings "He Hideth My Soul")

Not found in *101* or *101 More Hymn Stories*
See page 24 in *Amazing Grace*

Drama 15

He Leadeth Me

4 Characters: 2 Readers, Joseph Gilmore, Mrs. Gilmore

(Instruments begin by playing the refrain of "He Leadeth Me")

Reader 1: "He leadeth me, O blessed thought! O words with heav'nly comfort fraught!
Whate'er I do, where'er I be, still 'tis God's hand that leadeth me."

These words have been sung many times in church services since they were first written by Joseph Gilmore, an American Baptist pastor. They still speak to us today.

Reader 2: Joseph Gilmore was born in Boston, Massachusetts, in 1834. He served as pastor of several churches in the East and later taught Hebrew and English literature at Newton Seminary and Rochester University and wrote several college texts on these subjects. Although Gilmore was highly respected in his day in both religious and educational circles, today he is best remembered for this one hymn, hurriedly written when he was just 28 years of age.

Joseph Gilmore: "I had been speaking at the Wednesday evening service of the First Baptist Church in Philadelphia about the truths of the Twenty-third Psalm, and had been especially impressed with the blessedness of being led by God Himself. At the close of the service we adjourned to Deacon Watson's pleasant home where we were being entertained. During our conversation the wonder and blessedness of God's leading so grew upon me that I took out my pencil, wrote the text just as it stands today, handed it to my wife, and thought no more of it."

Mrs. Gilmore: "Without my husband's knowledge, I sent the quickly written text to the *Watchman and Reflector Magazine*, where it first appeared the following year. You can imagine my husband's surprise when he discovered his own hymn text already in print."

Joseph Gilmore: "Three years later I went to Rochester, New York, to preach as a candidate for the Second Baptist Church. Upon entering the chapel I took up a hymnal, thinking, 'I wonder what they sing here.' To my amazement the book opened up at 'He Leadeth Me,' and that was the first time I knew that my words had found a place among the songs of the church."

Reader 1:   The composer of the music for "He Leadeth Me" was William Bradbury, an important contributor to early gospel hymnody in this country. Mr. Bradbury has also supplied the music for such other favorites as—

Reader 2:   "Just As I Am," "The Solid Rock," "Savior, Like a Shepherd Lead Us," "Sweet Hour of Prayer," and many more.

Reader 1:   William Bradbury discovered Joseph Gilmore's text in the *Watchman and Reflector Magazine* and composed a fitting melody to match the words. Bradbury also added these lines to provide the refrain for the hymn—

Reader 2:   "His faithful follow'r I would be, for by His hand He leadeth me."

Reader 1:   When the First Baptist Church building of Philadelphia was demolished in 1926, it was replaced at the busy Broad and Arch intersection by a large new office building with a prominent bronze tablet containing the words for the first stanza of "He Leadeth Me." The inscription stated . . .

Reader 2:   "This is in recognition of the beauty and fame of the beloved hymn, and in remembrance of its distinguished author."

Reader 1:   Perhaps more than any other of our time, this hymn has been translated into many different languages. It is often one of the first hymns that missionaries translate into a native tongue. Servicemen during World War II were greatly surprised to find "He Leadeth Me" widely sung by the primitive Polynesians in the South Pacific. Like the Twenty-third Psalm on which it is based, the hymn meets a very basic and universal need in the lives of God's children everywhere—assurance of the Lord's guidance for every decision and crisis in life.

(Instruments begin playing softly)

* * * *

Reader 2:   While through this changing world below
I would not choose my path to go;
'Tis Father's hand that leadeth me,
Then O how safe His child must be.

Reader 1:   Why should I mind the way I go?
His way is best for me, I know.
He is my strength, my truth, my way,
He is my comfort, rod, and stay.

Reader 2:   So on we travel hand in hand,
Bound for the heavenly promised land;
Always through all eternity,
I'll praise His name for leading me.

(Author unknown)

Reader 1:   One of the thrilling blessings of the Christian life is the assurance that each day is a new faith adventure with God, realizing with childlike trust that our sovereign Heavenly Father will personally guide each step we take.

Reader 2:   Then we can move out with confidence with these reassuring words on our lips . . .

Joseph Gilmore: ⎱
Mrs. Gilmore: ⎰   "FOR BY HIS HAND HE LEADETH ME."

* * * *

(Congregation sings "He Leadeth Me")

See page 86, *101 Hymn Stories*

He Lives

3 Characters: 2 Readers, Alfred H. Ackley

Reader 1: "Why should I worship a dead Jew?"
Reader 2: This challenging question was posed by a sincere young Jewish student who had been attending evangelistic meetings conducted by the author and composer of this favorite hymn—

(Instruments play a portion of "He Lives")

Reader 1: Alfred H. Ackley's emphatic answer to this searching question came quickly . . .
Alfred H. Ackley: "He lives! I tell you, He is not dead, but lives here and now! Jesus Christ is more alive today than ever before. I can prove it by my own experience, as well as the testimony of countless thousands."
Reader 1: The young Jewish student eventually accepted the Living Christ as his own personal Savior. This experience inspired Mr. Ackley to begin reading the gospel accounts of the resurrection with fresh insights. The words "He is risen" suddenly had new meaning for him.
Reader 2: Soon Alfred Ackley expressed in song the thrill within his own soul.
Alfred H. Ackley: "The thought of His ever-living presence brought the words and music promptly and easily."
Reader 1: And since its first publication in 1933, "He Lives" continues to inspire Christian people with the truth that one of the most compelling proofs of the resurrection is the daily demonstration by believers that Christ's divine life is now being lived out in our very bodies— "HE LIVES WITHIN MY HEART!"
Reader 2: "I know that my Redeemer lives: What comfort this sweet sentence gives! He lives, He lives, who once was dead; He lives, my everlasting Head."

(Samuel Medley)

Reader 1: The names of the two Ackley brothers, Alfred and Benton, have been very prominent in gospel music. Both were long-time associates with the Rodeheaver Publishing Company, and each contributed many fine songs to various publications.

Reader 2:   Alfred Ackley, author and composer of "He Lives," received a thorough education in music, including study in composition at the Royal Academy of Music in London, England. As a performer, he was recognized as an accomplished cellist.

Reader 1:   Following graduation from the Westminster Theological Seminary, Alfred was ordained to the Presbyterian ministry. Even while pastoring churches in Pennsylvania and California, Pastor Ackley maintained a keen interest in the writing of gospel music.

Reader 2:   It is estimated that Ackley wrote more than 1,000 gospel songs before his home-going at the age of 73.

(Instruments begin playing softly)

✳   ✳   ✳   ✳

Reader 1:   But the one song for which the Christian church will ever be grateful to Alfred H. Ackley is this triumphant message that thrills our hearts and silences the scoffer with these words of personal experience—

Alfred H. Ackley: "YOU ASK ME HOW I KNOW HE LIVES? HE LIVES WITHIN MY HEART!"

Reader 1:   Then each believer can further say with a conviction based on the authority of God's Word itself—

Reader 2:   "I have been crucified with Christ and I no longer live, *but Christ lives in me.* The life I live in the body, I live by faith in the Son of God, who loved me and gave Himself for me" (Galatians 2:20).

✳   ✳   ✳   ✳

(Congregation sings "He Lives")

See page 115, *101 More Hymn Stories*

Hold the Fort

3 Characters: 3 Readers

(Instruments begin by playing the chorus of "Hold the Fort")

Reader 1:   At a YMCA conference in the year 1870, Major Daniel Whittle, a former officer in the Civil War, preached a stirring sermon from Revelation 2:25—

Reader 2:   "Only hold on to what you have until I come."

Reader 1:   Major Whittle then used an illustration from his war experience to close the message—

Reader 2:   A small force of Northern soldiers in charge of guarding a great quantity of supplies at the Allatoona Pass was besieged and hard pressed by greatly superior Confederate forces. Finally General French, the Confederate leader, commanded the Federal troops to surrender. At that moment on a hill some distance away the Northern leader, General Sherman, flashed a signal to his troops—

Reader 3:   "Hold the fort, I am coming. Sherman."

Reader 1:   In the audience that night when Major Whittle told this story was Philip P. Bliss, a well-known writer of early gospel music.

Reader 2:   The account so captivated Bliss that he could not sleep that evening until he had completed both the text and the music for a new song, "Hold the Fort." At the next day's YMCA service, Bliss introduced his rousing new gospel hymn to the delegates. The response was immediate and enthusiastic.

Reader 1:   "Hold the Fort" later became a great favorite in the Moody-Sankey campaigns in the United States and in Great Britain.

Reader 2:   During a Moody-Sankey campaign in the British Isles in 1874, Lord Shaftesbury, an esteemed Christian statesman, announced to the audience at the closing service . . .

Reader 3:   "If Mr. Sankey has done no more than teach our people to sing 'Hold the Fort,' he has conferred inestimable blessing on the British Empire, and it would have been worth all the expense of these meetings."

Reader 1: God calls each believer to a life of obedience and faithfulness in the place He has chosen for him—whether the tasks be great or small.

Reader 2: We also have a commander in heaven who has promised to return for us. Victory is certain. Our present responsibility, however, is to faithfully "hold the fort"— to "occupy till He comes" (Luke 19:13 KJV).

Reader 1: It is tragic, however, that many of God's people often develop negative attitudes of self-pity and apathy while serving their Lord.

Reader 2: "I've taught a class for many years;
Borne many burdens, toiled through tears—
But folks don't notice me a bit—
I'm so discouraged, I'll just quit.

I've led young people day and night,
And sacrificed to lead them right;
But folks won't help me out a bit—
And I'm so tired; I think I'll quit.

Reader 3: Christ's cause is hindered everywhere,
And people are dying in despair;
The reason why? Just think a bit—
The church is full of those who quit.
                              (Author unknown)

Reader 1: Before his tragic death at the early age of 38, Philip Bliss contributed other fine gospel hymns that are still much enjoyed: "My Redeemer," "Hallelujah, What a Savior," "Jesus Loves Even Me," "Wonderful Words of Life," "Almost Persuaded," and many more.

Reader 2: Even though Philip P. Bliss never considered today's hymn to be one of his better songs, his monument at Rome, Pennsylvania, bears this inscription—

Reader 3: "P.P. Bliss, author of 'Hold the Fort.'"

(Congregation sings "Hold the Fort")

See page 92, *101 Hymn Stories*

How Firm a Foundation

3 Characters: 3 Readers

Reader 1:   Many of our finest hymns are actually the truths and promises of Scripture set to music. For this service we are featuring one that has been a stalwart hymn of the church for more than 200 years.

Reader 2:   And still today we are spiritually refreshed each time we sing the biblical promises contained in this inspiring hymn—

(Instruments play a verse of "How Firm a Foundation"
—"Foundation" Tune)

Reader 1:   The authorship of this stirring hymn, "How Firm a Foundation," has always been a mystery to students of hymnody. Its first appearance was in 1787 in a hymnal titled *A Selection of Hymns from the Best Authors,* collected and published by Dr. John Rippon, a noted evangelical pastor of the Carter's Lane Baptist Church in London, England.

Reader 2:   The music generally used with this text is known as the "Foundation" tune and is an early American southern folk melody.

Reader 1:   Dr. Rippon was pastor of this well-known Baptist church in England for 63 years and was considered one of the most popular and influential dissenting ministers of his time. The hymn appeared anonymously in Pastor Rippon's hymn collection with the author indicated merely as "K."

Reader 2:   Since the music director in Dr. Rippon's church was named "Keene," it has been assumed that Mr. Keene is the "K" or author indicated in our hymnals.

Reader 1:   Like so many of our enduring hymns, "How Firm a Foundation" is really a sermon in song. In the first stanza the sure foundation of the Christian faith is established as being the Word of God itself, with this challenging question posed . . .

Reader 2:   What more can God do than give us His very Word as the completed revelation of Himself to man?

Reader 3:   "How firm a foundation, ye saints of the Lord, is laid for your faith in His excellent Word. What more can He say than to you He hath said—to you, who for refuge to Jesus have fled?"

Reader 1:   The succeeding verses then personalize and amplify precious promises that God has documented in His Word.

Reader 2:   The second stanza is a comforting promise found in Isaiah 41:10—"Fear thou not, for I am with thee, be not dismayed, for I am thy God."

Reader 3:   "Fear not, I am with thee—O be not dismayed, for I am thy God, I will still give thee aid; I'll strengthen thee, help thee, and cause thee to stand, upheld by My gracious, omnipotent hand."

Reader 1:   The third stanza recalls a precious promise especially for those passing through some deep crisis of life.

Reader 2:   This promise is found in Isaiah 43:2—"When you pass through the waters, I will be with you."

Reader 3:   "When thru the deep waters I call thee to go, the rivers of sorrow shall not overflow; for I will be with thee thy troubles to bless, and sanctify to thee thy deepest distress."

Reader 1:   The fourth stanza is based on a New Testament promise found in 2 Corinthians 12:9—

Reader 2:   "My grace is sufficient for you; for My strength is made perfect in weakness."

Reader 3:   "When thru fiery trials thy pathway shall lie, My grace, all-sufficient, shall be thy supply. The flame shall not hurt thee—I only design thy dross to consume and thy gold to refine."

Reader 1:   Then that powerful fifth stanza is based on one of the most glorious promises in Scripture. It is taken from Hebrews 13:5—

Reader 2:   "Never will I leave you; never will I forsake you!"

Reader 3:   "The soul that on Jesus hath leaned for repose, I will not, I will not desert to his foes; that soul, tho all hell should endeavor to shake, I'll never, no never—no never forsake."

Reader 2:   These are truly wonderful promises for us as be-lievers to appropriate. It is not surprising that those who do not have a personal faith in God such as this find it difficult to cope with the tensions of modern living and often must resort to chemical dependency to make it through another stressful day.

Reader 1:   As children of God we need to learn the lesson of daily "leaning for repose" upon the never-failing arms of our God and to remember the faithful promises of His Word whenever the difficulties of life cross our pathways.

(Instruments play softly while poem is read)

✳   ✳   ✳   ✳

Reader 3:   If the path I walk seems steep and rugged,
And I must labor long to reach the goal,
There's always One close by my side to help me;
He brings sweet rest and comfort to my soul.
And from the pages of God's Book before me,
He speaks the words that all my fears dispel,
And though I do not know the why nor wherefore,
I can be sure that He does all things well.

(Author unknown)

✳   ✳   ✳   ✳

*(Congregation sings "How Firm a Foundation"
—"Foundation" tune)*

See page 96, *101 Hymn Stories*

How Great Thou Art

3 Characters : 3 Readers

Reader 1:   A most challenging book entitled *Your God Is Too Small* tells of a group of Sunday school children who were asked to write down their ideas as to what God is like. The typical answer was: "God is a very old gentleman living somewhere up in space." The author, J. B. Phillips, goes on to point out the limited and immature views of the Almighty that even adults often have—that He is simply a benevolent father, or merely an ultimate escape from trouble when all else fails.

Reader 2:   The Prophet Isaiah also pondered the ageless question about the nature and character of God when he wrote in chapter 40—

Reader 3:   "To whom, then, will you compare God? What can you put beside Him? A metal image—that the workman casts? Can you not understand that He sits over the round earth so that its inhabitants look like grasshoppers; He spreads the skies out like a curtain, and stretches them like a tent. To whom will you compare Me? asks the Majestic One. Have you not heard that the Eternal is an everlasting God, the maker of the world from end to end?" (Isaiah 40:18-28).

Reader 2:   With the psalmist David we simply must conclude that . . .

Reader 3:   "The Lord is great and most worthy of praise: His greatness no one can fathom" (Psalm 145:3).

(Instruments play the chorus of "How Great Thou Art")

Reader 1:   "How Great Thou Art" is one of the hymnal's finest expressions for impressing us with God's greatness and majesty both in creation and redemption. If we are to truly worship God and trust Him with our lives, we must begin with a recognition of who He is and the knowledge of His limitless power.

Reader 2:   Although it was written in the past century, "How Great Thou Art" has only become familiar to congregations since the close of World War II. In a poll conducted some years ago by the *Christian Herald Magazine,* this inspiring song of praise was named the number one favorite hymn in America.

Reader 1:   The hymn was first introduced to American audiences at the Stony Brook Bible Conference in Long Island, New York, in the early 1950s. However, the hymn did not become a universal favorite until Cliff Barrows and "Bev" Shea of the Billy Graham Evangelistic Team used it during the London Crusade in the mid-1950's and again in the New York Crusade in 1957.

Reader 2:   A Swedish pastor, the Rev. Carl Boberg, was inspired to write this text after a visit to a beautiful country estate on the Southeast coast of Sweden in 1886. He recalled . . .

Reader 3:   "I was suddenly caught in a mid-day thunderstorm with awe-inspiring moments of flashing violence which were followed by a clear, brilliant sun. Soon afterwards I heard the calm, sweet songs of the birds in nearby trees. I was so overwhelmed by this display of nature that I fell to my knees in humble adoration to the mighty God of creation. In my exaltation I penned a nine-stanza poem with each stanza beginning with the Swedish words for 'O Great God.'"

Reader 2:   Several years later Pastor Boberg was attending a meeting in the Province of Varmland (VARM-lund), Sweden, and was greatly surprised to hear this congregation using an old Swedish folk melody for his words.

Reader 1:   After Pastor Boberg had written his poem, it was translated into the German language. Then the first literal English translation was made by the Rev. E. Gustav Johnson, a teacher from North Park College in Chicago, Illinois. This literal translation of Boberg's original poem was titled "O Mighty God, When I Behold the Wonder." These words are still found in some hymnals—

Reader 3:   "O mighty God, when I behold the wonder of nature's beauty, wrought by words of Thine, and how Thou leadest all from realms up yonder, sustaining earthly life in love benign, with rapture filled, my soul Thy name would laud, O mighty God, O mighty God!"

Reader 2:   About that same time another individual discovered the German version and translated it into the Russian language. It soon became especially popular with a group of Ukrainian believers.

Reader 1:   One day while two English missionaries, the Rev. and Mrs. Stuart K. Hine, were ministering in Russia, they heard a group of Ukrainians singing this lovely hymn with great enthusiasm. The Hines were so impressed by what they believed was an original Russian folk hymn that Rev. Hines began translating this Russian version into English.

Reader 2:   When World War II broke out in 1939, however, this missionary couple had to leave Russia and return to England with just the first three translated stanzas of what they considered to be a Russian folk hymn. It was not until after the close of the war in 1945 that Rev. Stuart Hine completed his translation of the thrilling final stanza, which reminds us that our great God will one day return to earth for His bride—believers from every age and culture—that they might sing of His greatness throughout all eternity.

(Instruments begin playing softly)

✳   ✳   ✳   ✳

Reader 1:   May our voices ring out with conviction now and throughout the ages to come . . .

Reader 3:   "O LORD MY GOD, HOW GREAT THOU ART!"

✳   ✳   ✳   ✳

(Congregation sings "How Great Thou Art")

See page 98, *101 Hymn Stories*

I Need Thee Every Hour

3 Characters: 2 Readers, Annie Hawks

Reader 1: To overcome the stress and strain of daily living, a Christian must have a sensitive awareness each day of receiving renewed strength from the Lord. Our featured hymn for this service has reminded God's people of this important truth for more than a century.

(Instruments play the chorus of "I Need Thee Every Hour")

Reader 1: This deeply personal hymn, "I Need Thee Every Hour", was written by a busy housewife and mother, Annie Hawks.

Reader 2: Annie Sherwood Hawks was born in Hoosick (HOOS-ick), New York, in 1835. At a very early age, she evidenced a gift for writing verse and at 14 was contributing poetry regularly to various newspapers. Although she wrote more than 400 poems, this hymn text is the only one still well-known.

Reader 1: At the age of 24, Annie Sherwood married Charles Hawks, and three children were born into this home. For much of her life Annie lived in Brooklyn, New York, and was a member of the Hanson Place Baptist Church, where Dr. Robert Lowry, a prominent gospel poet and musician, was the pastor.

Reader 2: Pastor Lowry recognized Mrs. Hawks' poetic gifts and encouraged her to use these talents in writing hymn texts.

Annie Hawks: "One day as a young wife and mother of 37 years of age, I was busy with my regular household tasks during a bright June morning in 1872. Suddenly, I became filled with the sense of nearness to the Master, and I began to wonder how anyone could ever live without Him, either in joy or pain. Then the words were ushered into my mind and these thoughts took full possession of me—

(Instruments play softly while words are read)

* * * *

I need Thee ev'ry hour, most gracious Lord; no tender
   voice like Thine can peace afford.
I need Thee ev'ry hour, stay Thou near by; temptations
   lose their pow'r when Thou art nigh.
I need Thee ev'ry hour, in joy or pain; come quickly
   and abide or life is vain.
I need Thee ev'ry hour, most Holy One; O make me
   Thine indeed, Thou blessed Son."

* * * *

Reader 1:   A short time later, Mrs. Hawks showed these verses
to Pastor Robert Lowry, who was much impressed with
them. Lowry quickly composed the music for the text
and also added the refrain—"I need Thee, O I need
Thee, ev'ry hour I need Thee! O bless me now, my
Savior—I come to Thee!"

Reader 2:   Dr. Lowry always had the conviction that any gospel hymn should have a refrain or chorus to give it
completeness as well as to provide an opportunity for
everyone, especially the children, to share in the singing.

Reader 1:   From the pen of this dedicated pastor-musician came
other favorite hymns—

Reader 2:   "Christ Arose," "Nothing But the Blood," "Shall
We Gather at the River?" and the stirring music for
"We're Marching to Zion."

Reader 1:   Sixteen years after writing her hymn text, Mrs.
Hawks experienced the death of her husband.

Reader 2:   During this difficult period of her life, she was surprised at the spiritual help she received from her own
hymn:

Annie Hawks: "I did not understand at first why this hymn
had touched the great throbbing heart of humanity. It
was not until long after, when the shadow fell over my
way, that shadow of great loss, that I understood something of the comforting power in the words which I
had been permitted to give out to others in my hour of
sweet serenity and peace."

Reader 1: One of the thrilling blessings of being a Christian is the possibility of knowing the closeness of God in every situation of life. Like Annie Hawks, it is important that we develop strong spritiual lives during the joyful, peaceful hours so that we will be able to remain steadfast when difficulties come. The Scriptures teach that in every life there will be times of laughter and times of weeping . . . (Ecclesiastes 3:1-8). Regardless of the circumstances, we must live each day in the spirit of complete dependence on our Lord, with an awareness that He is equally at work in our lives during periods of "joy or pain."

(Instruments begin playing softly)

✳ ✳ ✳ ✳

Reader 2: As we sing these words written by Annie Hawks more than a century ago, may they truly reflect our own attitude . . .

Annie Hawks: "I NEED THEE—EV'RY HOUR I NEED THEE!—MOST GRACIOUS LORD."

✳ ✳ ✳ ✳

(Congregation sings "I Need Thee Every Hour")

See page 132, *101 More Hymn Stories*

• "I thank God for my handicaps, for, through them, I have found myself, my work, and my God."
                                                           —Helen Keller

Drama 21

In the Garden

4 Characters: 3 Readers, C. Austin Miles

Reader 1: One of the most thrilling and dramatic scenes of Scripture is recorded in the 20th chapter of John's gospel. Early on that Sunday morning after Christ's crucifixion while it was still dark, Mary Magdalene quietly made her way to the tomb. She was startled to find that the stone had been removed from the entrance.

Reader 2: Hurriedly Mary went to tell Peter and John this shocking news! The two men raced for the tomb and went in but discovered only the grave clothes of their Lord.

Reader 1: Amazed, they returned quickly to their homes to tell the other disciples what they had seen while Mary remained outside the empty tomb quietly weeping.

Reader 2: Suddenly she was startled by the voices of two angels in white asking why she was crying.

Reader 3: "They have taken my Lord away, and I don't know where they have put Him."

Reader 1: Then through her tears she saw another figure behind her who asked: "Woman, why are you crying?"

Reader 2: Thinking that this was merely the gardener, Mary pleaded somewhat indignantly—

Reader 3: "Sir, if you have carried Him away, tell me where you have put Him, and I will get Him."

Reader 1: Then the Lord spoke gently—"Mary."

Reader 2: One can well imagine the excitement in her voice when she responded—

Reader 3: "Rabboni!" ("My Master"). (John 20:1-18)

Reader 1: This thrilling biblical account became the basis for this hymn, one of the most popular gospel songs ever written—

(Instruments play a portion of "In the Garden")

Reader 2: It was in 1912 that music publisher Dr. Adam Geibel (GI-bul) asked author and composer C. Austin Miles to write a text that would be "sympathetic in tone, breathing tenderness in every line, one that would bring hope to the hopeless, rest for the weary, and downy pillows to dying beds."

C. Austin Miles: "One day in March, 1912, I was seated in the dark room where I kept my photographic equipment and organ. I drew my Bible toward me; it opened at my favorite chapter, John 20—whether by chance or inspiration let each reader decide. That meeting of Jesus and Mary had lost none of its power and charm. As I read it that day, I seemed to be part of the scene. I became a silent witness to that dramatic moment in Mary's life when she knelt before her Lord and cried, 'Rabboni!'

My hands were resting on the Bible while I stared at the light blue wall. As light faded, I seemed to be standing at the entrance of the garden, looking down a gently winding path, shaded by olive branches. A woman in white, with head bowed, hand clasping her throat as if to choke back her sobs, walked slowly into the shadows. It was Mary. As she came to the tomb, upon which she placed her hand, she bent over to look in, and hurried away.

John in flowing robe appeared, looking at the tomb; then came Peter, who entered the tomb, followed slowly by John.

As they departed, Mary reappeared; leaning her head upon her arm at the tomb, she wept. Turning herself, she saw Jesus standing; so did I. I knew it was He. She knelt before Him with arms outstretched and looking into His face cried, 'Rabboni!'

I awakened in full light, gripping the Bible, with muscles tense and nerves vibrating. Under the inspiration of this vision I wrote as quickly as the words could be formed—the poem exactly as it has since appeared. That same evening I composed the music."

(Instruments begin playing softly)

＊　＊　＊　＊

Reader 1:   Though it is always thrilling to recall the dramatic
events of that first Easter Sunday, the celebration of a
risen, reigning Savior must be a renewing personal experience in each believer's daily life, always causing us
"to triumph in Christ" (2 Corinthians 2:14 KJV).

Reader 2:   May the singing of this beloved hymn remind us
anew that the resurrected Christ still desires to share
His life with His followers—to walk and talk with us
and to fill our lives each day with His power and joy.

＊　＊　＊　＊

(Congregation sings "In the Garden")

See page 124, *101 Hymn Stories*

• They came to the quiet garden
In the early morning gloom,
And there in the shadowed darkness
They found an empty tomb.

Their hearts were heavy laden,
Bowed down with deep despair;
But when they lifted tear-dimmed eyes,
Lo, Jesus was standing there.

So oft in the midst of sorrows
When hope seems cold and dead,
With lifted eyes, we too may see
An empty tomb instead.

—Author unknown

It Is Well with My Soul

3 Characters: 2 Readers, Philip P. Bliss

Reader 1:   A new style of sacred music known as the "gospel song" appeared during the last half of the nineteenth century. This type of music developed with the ministries of Christian leaders like Dwight L. Moody, who conducted city-wide evangelistic crusades in the United States and Great Britain.

Reader 2:   Ira Sankey, Mr. Moody's song leader and associate for nearly 30 years, described this new style of sacred music as songs that were "calculated to awaken the careless, to melt the hardened, and to guide inquiring souls to Jesus Christ." Many of these songs were written as a result of some sudden inspiration or after a dramatic human experience.

Reader 1:   A gospel song of this type is our featured hymn for this service. The words grew out of a series of bitter hardships and tragedies suffered by the author, Horatio Spafford. It is a hymn that still expresses well the personal testimony of every devout believer.

(Instruments play a portion of "It Is Well with My Soul")

Reader 1:   The music for this familiar and well-loved gospel hymn, "It Is Well with My Soul," was composed by Philip P. Bliss, a noted gospel song writer, musician and a member of the Moody-Sankey evangelistic team. He recalls the events that inspired the song—

Philip P. Bliss: "Many wonderful associations with friends who supported our evangelistic work developed as time went on. One such individual who contributed generously to the campaigns, both spiritually and financially, was Horatio Spafford, a very successful attorney and businessman here in Chicago, a devout Christian and a faithful member of the Presbyterian Church. He and I became very close friends. One of the saddest memories of my life was that November

22nd in 1873 when our Chicago papers carried these shocking headlines:"

Reader 2: "The tragic shipwreck of the S.S. *Ville De Havre* today claimed the lives of four daughters of Chicago's prominent attorney, Horatio Spafford. Only his wife saved—now in Cardiff, Wales. Hundreds more lost at sea. City mourns this tragedy."

Reader 1: The Spaffords had five lovely children. Two years earlier, their only son became ill and with very little warning died suddenly. Then a short time later a devastating fire broke out in Chicago, destroying much of the Lake Michigan shoreline property, including most of Mr. Spafford's extensive real estate investments.

Reader 2: About this same time, Mr. Moody and Ira Sankey left for Great Britain to conduct another evangelistic campaign. Desiring to assist them with this endeavor and hoping that his saddened family might be encouraged by such a trip, Horatio made arrangements for all of his family to sail to Europe. At the last minute, however, some unexpected urgent business matters detained him. He sent on as scheduled his wife and four daughters—Tanetta, Maggie, Annie and Bessie—promising to join them as soon as possible.

Reader 1: Several days after their departure, Spafford completed his business affairs and eagerly prepared to rejoin his family in Europe. As he was busily packing, there was a knock at the door and he was handed a cable which read simply—"SAVED ALONE. YOUR WIFE."

Reader 2: The newspapers that day provided the tragic details: The ship had been struck by another vessel. It sank in twelve minutes with all four of Spafford's daughters drowned, along with more than 200 other passengers. Mrs. Spafford had miraculously escaped and was now waiting for her grief-stricken husband to join her in Cardiff, Wales.

Philip P. Bliss: "Not long after arriving in Wales, Horatio wrote me a letter. He related that he had stayed on the deck of the ship hour after hour watching the rolling waves and grieving the loss of his four precious daughters. When the ship passed somewhere near the area very likely where the drownings had occurred, some poetic thoughts began to shape themselves in his mind. He had an overwhelming sense of God's presence about him and felt his soul strangely comforted as he meditated on the redemptive work of Christ and the promise of His return."

Reader 1:   Later Mr. Spafford asked Philip Bliss to look over the lines he had written to see if they might lend themselves to a song.

Philip P. Bliss: "I began working immediately on a singable tune for his unusual text, all the time praying earnestly that this hymn would be a source of much comfort to the Spaffords as well as to others in their times of stress and grief. Soon I was able to sing . . ." (music begins)

(Soloist and congregation [refrain] sing "It Is Well with My Soul")

See page 126, *101 Hymn Stories*

Drama 23

Jesus, Lover of My Soul

3 Characters: 2 Readers, Charles Wesley

Reader 1: Charles Wesley is one of the best known of all hymn writers. He is often called the "sweet bard of Methodism." Our featured hymn for the service today is just one of more than 6500 hymns written by this noted eighteenth century author. Scarcely a day passed in which Charles Wesley did not fashion some routine happening into a lofty expression of spiritual truth related to the Christian experience. Our hymnals still contain these Wesley favorites—

Reader 2: "O for a Thousand Tongues"; "And Can It Be?"; "Hark, the Herald Angels Sing"; "Christ the Lord Is Risen Today"; "Soldiers of Christ Arise"; "A Charge to Keep I Have"; and "Jesus, Lover of My Soul."

(Instruments play one stanza of "Jesus, Lover of My Soul"—
"Martyn" Tune)

Reader 1: "Jesus, Lover of My Soul" is generally regarded as one of the finest of all the Wesleyan hymns. It was first published in 1740.

Reader 2: And more than 250 years later it has been translated into almost every known language and is still found in nearly every published hymnal.

Reader 1: Charles Wesley was born at Epworth, England in 1707. He was next to the youngest of 19 children born to Samuel Wesley and his remarkable wife Susanna. The Wesley family was one of the most distinguished in England in that day. Their great-grandfather and grandfather were both Oxford graduates and Church of England clergymen. The father, Samuel Wesley, was also a clergyman of the Anglican Church in the parish at Epworth.

Reader 2: However, the care of the 13 children who survived beyond infancy was no easy task for a minister with a small parish salary. On at least one occasion Samuel

Wesley was imprisoned because of his inability to pay his debts.

Reader 1:   Yet in spite of poverty, sickness and harrassment from their rough Epworth neighbors, the Wesley household was a happy and harmonious one, a notable accomplishment in a family of such size. Susanna Wesley, the real strength of this family, was always very attentive to the spiritual as well as the physical and social needs of each member of her family. It is said that she scheduled one hour a week with each child to lead them in personal Bible study in addition to the daily family devotions.

Reader 2:   Charles received a thorough education from his mother and later at the Westminster School of London, where his older brother Samuel was the head-master. At the age of 19 Charles entered Oxford University. Upon graduation he received Holy Orders from the Anglican church and soon sailed for America to be the personal secretary to the governor of Georgia and to assist his older brother John in evangelizing the American Indians. This experience, however, proved to be disappointing, and within a short time both John and Charles returned to England, discouraged and broken in spirit.

Reader 1:   Soon after his return to England, Charles attended a meeting of a small group of devout Moravian believers in the Aldersgate Hall in London. Charles described the event in his journal:

Charles Wesley: "At midnight I gave myself to Christ, assured that I was safe, whether sleeping or waking. I had the continual experience of His power to overcome all temptation, and I confessed with joy and surprise that He was able to do exceedingly abundantly for me, above what I could ask or think."

Reader 2:   "Jesus, Lover of My Soul" is thought to have been written by Charles Wesley soon after this "heart-warming" Aldersgate experience. Then John, too, had a similar experience. Though both brothers had been taught and had even preached the truths of being rightly related to God through faith in Christ, their new-found spiritual relationship with the Lord became very personal and dynamic for them. Together they began a fruitful evangelistic ministry throughout Great Britain. Their zealous activities eventually led to the founding of the world-wide Methodist denomination.

Reader 1:   Various accounts have been given of a possible event that might have prompted Charles Wesley to write this hymn text, though none has ever been completely authenticated.

Reader 2:   One account states that on his return to England in the fall of 1736, following his disappointing experience in the United States, Charles was caught in a frightening storm at sea when it appeared for certain that all would be lost. When the ship finally reached land, Wesley wrote in his journal for that date . . .

Charles Wesley: "I knelt down and blessed the hand that had conducted me through such inextricable (tangled) mazes."

Reader 2:   During this storm it is said that a frightened bird flew into Wesley's cabin and sheltered itself in his bosom for comfort and safety, and it was this memory that inspired the writing of the hymn a short time later.

Reader 1:   Another account suggests that Charles wrote this text while lying under an English hedgerow, having been beaten by an angry mob that opposed the evangelical emphasis of the Wesleys' ministry.

Reader 2:   Still others see this text simply as an expression of Charles Wesley's personal struggle to find peace with the Almighty prior to his surrender to God and the transforming Aldersgate experience.

Reader 1:   Even though its origin remains an uncertainty, many have called this the "finest heart-hymn in the English language." The meaningful simplicity of the text is its special appeal. It is interesting to note that 156 of the 188 words are common one-syllable words. Also noteworthy is the exaltation of Christ. He is presented with such picturesque terms as . . .

Reader 2:   "Lover," "healer," "refuge," "fountain," "wing," and "pilot"—the all-sufficient One!

Reader 1:   And truly any believer who has experienced God's redeeming love and enjoyed the daily presence of an all-sufficient Lord must respond even as Charles Wesley did. . .

Charles Wesley: "Thou, O Christ, art all I want, more than all in Thee I find."

Reader 1:   Henry Ward Beecher, a noted American preacher of the past century, once paid this tribute to the hymn—

Reader 2:   "I would rather have written that hymn of Wesley's than to have the fame of all the kings that ever sat on the earth. It is more glorious and has more power in it. I would rather be the author of that hynm than to hold the wealth of the richest man in New York. He will die, but that hymn will go on singing until the last trump brings forth the angel band; and then, I think, it will mount up on some lips to the very presence of God."

(Instruments begin playing softly)

✻   ✻   ✻   ✻

Reader 1:   May we apply to our lives the truth of this hymn— the sufficiency of Christ for the present as well as the future—and then learn to rest daily in the enjoyment of His unfailing love.

Reader 2:   As we sing this ageless hymn, may these words by Charles Wesley truly express our earnest prayer—

Charles Wesley: "Thou of life the fountain art, freely let me take of Thee; spring Thou up within my heart, rise to all eternity."

✻   ✻   ✻   ✻

(Congregation sings, "Jesus, Lover of My Soul"—"Martyn" Tune)

See page 129, *101 Hymn Stories*

Drama 24

Jesus Loves Me

3 Characters: 3 Readers

Reader 1:   Some of our finest hymns were written especially for children. Christian leaders have long realized that music can be one of the most effective ways of impressing youth with spiritual truths.

Reader 2:   And without doubt the gospel song that has been sung more often by children than any other is this simply stated one written by Anna Warner in 1860.

(Instruments play a portion of "Jesus Loves Me")

Reader 1:   Although it is so familiar, we still enjoy hearing and singing this charming children's hymn—"Jesus Loves Me, This I Know." Miss Warner was assisted by her sister Susan in writing this text. It was part of their novel, *Say and Seal*, one of the best-selling books of that time although today there would be few individuals who would know or remember the plot of that story, which once stirred the hearts of many readers.

Reader 2:   But the simple poem spoken by one of the characters, Mr. Linden, as he comforts Johnny Fax, a dying child, still remains the favorite hymn of countless children around the world—

(Instruments play softly while words are read)

✳   ✳   ✳   ✳

Reader 3:   "1. Jesus loves me! This I know, for the Bible tells me so;
Little ones to Him belong; they are weak but He is strong.

2. Jesus loves me, loves me still tho' I'm very weak and ill;
That I might from sin be free, bled and died upon the tree.

3. Jesus loves me! He who died heaven's gate to
    open wide;
He will wash away my sin, let His little child come in.

4. Jesus loves me! He will stay close beside me all
    the way;
Thou hast bled and died for me; I will henceforth
live for Thee.
Yes, Jesus loves me! The Bible tells me so!"

✳ ✳ ✳ ✳

Reader 1: Anna and Susan Warner were both well educated and
deeply devoted Christian women. Their entire lives were
spent in a lovely secluded area along the Hudson River.

Reader 2: Their home was near the United States Military
Academy at West Point, New York, and for a number
of years these two sisters conducted Sunday school
classes for the young cadets. In recognition of their
spiritual contributions to our nation's young military
officers, both sisters were buried with military honors.

Reader 1: After the death of their parents, the two Warner
sisters were left with a rather meager income and of
necessity they began serious literary writing. Susan became highly recognized for several of her works, especially *The Wide, Wide World*, considered at that time to
be exceeded in popularity only by *Uncle Tom"s Cabin*.

Reader 2: In another of Susan Warner's works, *The Little Cor-
poral*, this familiar children's text appeared—

Reader 3: "Jesus bids us shine with a clear, pure light
Like a little candle burning in the night;
In the world is darkness, so we must shine,
You in your small corner, and I in mine."

Reader 1: Although she was not as well-known as Susan for her
literary fame, Anna Warner also wrote a number of novels
as well as two collections of sacred verse. Another of Anna's
fine hymn texts is still found in many hymnals—

Reader 3: "We would see Jesus, for the shadows lengthen
across the little landscapes of our lives;
We would see Jesus, our weak faith to strengthen for
the last weariness, the final strife."

Reader 2: William Bradbury, the composer of the music for "Jesus Loves Me," contributed much to early gospel hymnody in the United States. He was recognized as a pioneer in children's music in both the church and the public schools. Bradbury also composed the music for other well-known hymns, including . . .

Reader 3: "The Solid Rock," "Sweet Hour of Prayer," "He Leadeth Me," and "Just As I Am."

Reader 1: Although "Jesus Loves Me" was intended for children, its message is relevant for those of all ages.

Reader 2: It has been reported that a brilliant seminary professor always closed his final class each year with these words—

Reader 3: "Gentlemen, there is still much in this world and in the Bible that I do not understand, but of one thing I am certain—'Jesus loves me, this I know, for the Bible tells me so'—and gentlemen, that is sufficient!"

(Instruments begin playing softly)

❋ ❋ ❋ ❋

Reader 1: Children are the prized possessions of the church. The highest priority of any congregation should be the teaching and training of youngsters in the ways of God.

Reader 2: Christ was our example in His concern for children throughout His earthly ministry. In the midst of the pressures of ministering to the multitudes, He always had time to invite youngsters to Himself. One day the disciples rebuked those who had brought their children to the Lord. But when Jesus saw it, He was much displeased and taught them this pointed lesson—

Reader 3: "Let the little children come to Me, and do not hinder them, for the kingdom of God belongs to such as these. I tell you the truth, anyone who will not receive the kingdom of God like a little child will never enter it" (Luke 18:15-17).

❋ ❋ ❋ ❋

(Congregation sings "Jesus Loves Me")

See page 132, *101 Hymn Stories*

Jesus Paid It All

4 Characters: 2 Readers, Elvina Hall, Pastor George Schrick

Reader 1:   The emphasis of all the world's religions can be spelled with two letters—D–O. The Christian gospel, however, is spelled with four letters—D–O–N–E! Our featured hymn for this service reminds us clearly of this important truth—that our security in this life and our hope for eternity depend not on our own feeble efforts, but solely on Christ's finished work.

(Instruments play a verse of "Jesus Paid It All")

Reader 2:   This familiar gospel hymn, "Jesus Paid It All," was written by Elvina Hall one Sunday morning in the year 1865. As a member of the choir of the Monument Street Methodist Church in Baltimore, Maryland, she supposedly was listening to the sermon by her pastor, the Rev. George Schrick. Following the service, she approached her pastor timidly with a hymnal in her hand:

Elvina Hall: "Oh, Pastor Schrick, may I speak with you a moment?"

Pastor Schrick: "Good morning, Mrs. Hall. Say, that choir number was excellent this morning. Did you notice that it was right in line with my sermon?"

Elvina Hall: "Oh, pastor, I really must confess that I wasn't listening as closely as usual to your message this morning. Because, you see, once you started preaching about how we can really know God's love and forgiveness, I began thinking about all that Christ has already done to provide our salvation. Then these words came to me, and I just had to get them down on paper. But there I was in full view in the choir loft. So I just tore out the fly leaf of this hymnal and scribbled the words on that!"

Pastor Schrick: "Oh, Elvina, you might just have to pay for a new hymnal! *(laughing)* No, in fact, I firmly believe that when we allow God's Word to have an active place in our lives, it stimulates our creative abilities and makes it possible for the Holy Spirit to use our humble talents and bring spiritual blessing to others. It's very possible, Elvina, that God has touched your life in that way this morning."

Elvina Hall: *(Hesitantly)* "But I was wondering if you might have time to look at my verses . . ."

Pastor Schrick: "Well, I really should be on my way . . ."

Elvina Hall: *(Interrupting)* "Just to see what you think of them?"

Pastor Schrick: "Oh, all right . . . *(Pause)* Say, I like these lines . . . Now that reminds me of something else. A short time ago our good organist, John Grape, gave me a copy of a new tune that he had recently composed. Yes, here's a copy of the music right in my Bible. Elvina, you read that first stanza while I see if possibly John's tune might match your words—"

(Elvina reads the words of her first stanza while the notes of the melody are played on the piano)

Elvina Hall: "I hear the Savior say, 'Thy strength indeed is small!
Child of weakness, watch and pray; find in Me thine all in all.'"

Pastor Schrick: "Oh, that's wonderful, Elvina; the words that you wrote in the choir loft this morning fit perfectly with John Grape's new tune. Now read your other verses for me as well."

(Elvina reads the other verses)

Elvina Hall: "Lord, now indeed I find Thy pow'r, and Thine alone,
Can change the leper's spots and melt the heart of stone.

For nothing good have I whereby Thy grace to claim—
I'll wash my garments white in the blood of Calv'ry's Lamb.

And when before the throne I stand in Him complete,
'Jesus died my soul to save,' my lips shall still repeat."

Pastor Schrick: "Now all we need is a good refrain—something that will summarize all of those ideas into one strong final statement. Perhaps something like—Jesus paid it all . . ."

Elvina Hall: "All to Him I owe . . ."

Pastor Schrick: "Sin had left a crimson stain . . ."

Elvina Hall: "He washed it white as snow."

Reader 1: Mrs. Elvina Mabel Hall was born in 1820, in Alexandria, Virginia. Little is known of her life except that she and her husband were faithful members of the Monument Street Methodist Church in Baltimore for more than 40 years.

Reader 2: John Grape, composer of the tune, was a successful coal merchant in Baltimore, who, as he once stated, "dabbled in music for my own amusement." For many years he was an active layman in the Monument Street Church, working in the Sunday school as well as serving as the organist and choir director.

Reader 1: "Jesus Paid It All" first appeared in Philip Bliss' *Gospel Song Book Collection* in 1874, nine years after being written.

Reader 2: This hymn, hurriedly written by a lay woman, is still widely sung today, especially during communion services.

Elvina Hall: "I'm always amazed that God could use a simple housewife like me and a humble organist like John Grape, and of course an encouraging pastor like Rev. Schrick, to bring this hymn to people all over the world. You know, I think if God could use someone like me, He could use almost anyone—perhaps even you!"

(Congregation sings "Jesus Paid It All")

See page 160, *101 More Hymn Stories*

Joyful, Joyful, We Adore Thee

3 Characters: 2 Readers, Dr. Henry van Dyke

Reader 1: "The fruit of the Spirit is love, JOY . . . against such things there is no law" (Galatians 5:22).

Reader 2: Some say that the Bible contains little humor. Yet the subject of joy is given great importance in the Scriptures. Nehemiah 8:10 teaches that experiencing the joy of the Lord is the very basis of a believer's spiritual strength in daily living.

Reader 1: And from King Solomon comes this wise reminder: "A cheerful heart is good medicine, but a crushed spirit dries up the bones" (Proverbs 17:22). Christ Himself instructs us in John 15:11—"I have told you this so that My joy may be in you and that your joy may be complete."

Reader 2: Genuine joy is important not only for our own emotional and physical well-being, but also as an influence for God in all of our daily relationships, especially those with our non-Christian friends and colleagues.

Reader 1: At the close of each day, can we honestly say that we have tried to make it a pleasant experience for others to associate with us? Have we been enjoyable to be with?

(Instruments play a portion of "Joyful, Joyful, We Adore Thee")

Reader 2: "Joyful, Joyful, We Adore Thee" is one of the most triumphant hymns in the English language. Its author was a prominent Presbyterian minister named Henry van Dyke.

Reader 1: During his lifetime of 81 years, Henry van Dyke was recognized as one of the most talented Presbyterian preachers and leading literary figures in America. In addition to achieving fame as a minister, for a number of years he was a professor of literature at Princeton University. He also served as Moderator of his denomination, as a Navy chaplain during World War I, and as an ambassador to Holland and Luxembourg under President Wilson.

Reader 2: High honors in many different areas came to this distinguished man. He was a prolific and exceptional writer of devotional materials. Many of his books became best sellers, including the well-known *The Other Wise Man*.

Reader 1: Yet this one fine hymn, first published in 1911, is the work for which Henry van Dyke is probably best remembered today.

Reader 2: The text for "Joyful, Joyful, We Adore Thee" was written while Henry van Dyke was a guest minister at Williams College in Williamstown, Massachusetts. Dr. van Dyke was an ardent lover of nature. One morning he handed a poem to the college president with this remark—

Dr. Henry van Dyke: "Here is a new hymn for you. Your great Bershire (BERK-shur) Mountains have been my inspiration. It must be sung to the music of Beethoven's 'Hymn of Joy.'"

Reader 2: Later he shared his purpose for writing this hymn—

Dr. Henry van Dyke: "These verses are simple expressions of common Christian feelings and desires in this present time. This hymn may be sung together by people who know the thought of the age, and are not afraid that any truth of science will destroy their faith or that any revolution on earth will ever overthrow the Kingdom of Heaven. Therefore this is a hymn of trust and hope in God."

Reader 1: With his fine literary skills, Henry van Dyke created colorful impressions in this text—

Reader 2: In the first stanza, he expressed with imagery the joyful interplay between nature and believers as they both offer praise to their Creator.

Dr. Henry van Dyke: "Hearts unfold like flowers before Thee, hail Thee as the sun above."

Reader 1: Then the second verse reminds us that all of God's creation speaks of His glory, directing our response of praise to the Creator Himself . . .

Dr. Henry van Dyke: "All Thy works with joy surround Thee, call us to rejoice in Thee."

Reader 2: The third stanza is a personal challenge for believers living in God's created world . . .

Dr. Henry van Dyke: "Teach us how to love each other . . . lift us to the joy divine."

Reader 1: And the fourth stanza concludes with an invitation for all of God's children to join the mighty chorus of joy begun at Creation's dawn when the morning stars sang for joy as described in Job 38:7. With this attitude of joyous living we find the strength to be victorious in any circumstance of life.

Dr. Henry van Dyke: "Mortals, join the mighty chorus which the morning stars began . . . ever singing, march we onward, victors in the midst of strife."

Reader 2: The vibrant music for this hymn is adapted from the fourth movement of Beethoven's last symphony. This Ninth or Choral Symphony is generally considered to be the greatest of all his nine symphonies, even though it was written after Beethoven became totally deaf. It was the composer's desire to write a final symphony that would combine both instruments and voices in one majestic expression of sound.

(Instruments play softly to the end)

* * * *

Reader 1: To become a Christian is to receive a song for this life and for eternity—

Reader 2: "He put a new song in my mouth, a hymn of praise to our God" (Psalm 40:3).

Reader 1: This song of joyous praise should express our gratitude to God and in turn influence others for Him—

Reader 2: "I will praise God's name in song and glorify Him with thanksgiving . . ." "In the presence of the congregation I will sing Your praises" (Psalm 69:30; Hebrews 2:12).

Reader 1: God's people of every generation have been called to be people of joy, praise, and thanksgiving. They are to represent the character and worth of the Almighty—

to be living demonstrations for a defiled world of a victorious, joyful lifestyle.

Reader 2:   "For the kingdom of God is not a matter of eating and drinking, but of righteousness, peace and JOY in the Holy Spirit, because anyone who serves Christ in this way is pleasing to God and approved by men" (Romans 14:17, 18).

*   *   *   *

(Congregation sings "Joyful, Joyful, We Adore Thee")

See page 143, *101 Hymn Stories*

- "Joy is the health of the soul; sadness is its poison."
  —Author unknown

- "The Christian life that is joyless is a discredit to God and a disgrace to itself."   —Maltbie D. Babcock

- "Joy flourishes best in the garden of praise."
  —Author unknown

Drama 27

Just As I Am

4 Characters: 2 Readers, Charlotte Elliott, Pastor H.V. Elliott

(Instruments begin by playing one stanza of "Just As I Am")

Reader 1:   It is possible that more hearts have been touched and more people influenced for Christ by this one hymn, "Just As I Am," than by any other song ever written. Its text was born within the soul of an invalid woman named Charlotte Elliott as the result of intense feelings of uselessness and despair.

Reader 2:   As a young person Charlotte Elliott lived a carefree life in Brighton, England. She gained popularity as a portrait artist and a writer of humorous verse. When she was thirty, however, her health began to fail rapidly and she became an invalid for the remaining years of her life. She was extremely depressed. But a turning point in her life came when a noted Swiss evangelist, Dr. Ceasar Malan, visited the Elliott home. Counseling with Charlotte about her spiritual and emotional problems, the evangelist finally pleaded with her—

Reader 1:   "Charlotte, you must come just as you are, a sinner, to the Lamb of God who takes away the sin of the world. And if you will only come to Him, He'll surely forgive and receive you."

Reader 2:   Throughout the remainder of her life, every year Charlotte celebrated that day in 1822 when her Swiss friend had led her to a personal relationship with Christ. And though the text for "Just As I Am" was not written until 14 years later, it is apparent that Charlotte never forgot the words of Dr. Malan, for they form the very essence of this hymn's text.

Reader 1:   Charlotte Elliott lived to the age of 82, even though she was in ill health for more than 50 years. Often she endured times of great physical suffering—

Charlotte Elliott: "He knows, and He alone, what it is, day after day, hour after hour, to fight against bodily feelings of almost overpowering weakness, langour and exhaustion; to resolve not to yield to slothfulness, depression and instability, such as the body causes me to indulge, but to rise every morning determined to take for my motto: 'If a man will come after Me, let him deny himself, take up his cross daily, and follow Me.'"

Reader 2:   Charlotte Elliott wrote the text for "Just As I Am" in 1836. It was published that same year in the second edition of *The Invalid's Hymn Book,* a collection which contained 115 of her original works. Miss Elliott wrote approximately 150 hymns and is regarded today as one of the finest of all English hymn writers.

Charlotte Elliott: "I remember writing 'Just As I Am' . . . I was feeling particularly despondent and useless. I had been living with my brother, who was pastor of the parish church here in Brighton. He was busily engaged in trying to raise funds to build a badly needed new educational building in which to train the children of poor clergymen.

One day as my brother visited my bedside I exclaimed: 'I just feel so utterly useless while you and your parishioners are working so hard to get enough funds for that new building. I wish there was something that I could do to help instead of just lying here all the time.'"

Pastor H.V. Elliott: "Now, Charlotte, I don't want to hear you talking that way again. God has given you a very special talent for writing verses that have brought spiritual help to a great number of people through the years. By the way, didn't I see you working on a new poem this morning? Yes, here it is, right next to your bed. Read to me what you have written."

(Instruments play softly while words are read)

* * * *

Charlotte Elliott: 1. "Just as I am, without one plea but that Thy blood was shed for me, and that Thou bidd'st me come to Thee, O Lamb of God, I come, I come!

2. Just as I am, and waiting not to rid my
   soul of one dark blot, to Thee whose
   blood can cleanse each spot, O Lamb of
   God, I come, I come!
3. Just as I am, tho tossed about with
   many a conflict, many a doubt,
   fightings and fears within, without, O
   Lamb of God, I come, I come!
4 Just as I am, poor wretched, blind—
   sight, riches, healing of the mind, yea,
   all I need in Thee to find—O Lamb of
   God, I come, I come!
5 Just as I am, Thou wilt receive, wilt
   welcome, pardon, cleanse, relieve;
   because Thy promise I believe, O Lamb
   of God, I come, I come!
6. Just as I am, Thy love unknown has
   broken ev'ry barrier down; now to be
   Thine, yea, Thine alone, O Lamb of
   God, I come, I come!

✳ ✳ ✳ ✳

Reader 1: To her brother's amazement, when it was printed
and sold, this one poem from the pen of his invalid
sister brought in more funds for the new school building
than all of his parishioners' fund-raising projects. After
Charlotte's death there were found among her papers
more than 1,000 letters from individuals around the
world expressing gratitude for the spiritual influence of
this hymn in their lives.

Reader 2: Charlotte's pastor brother left this statement as he
approached retirement—

Pastor H.V. Elliott: "In the course of a long ministry I have
been permitted to see much fruit for my labors; but I
feel that more has been done for God's kingdom by this
single hymn of my sister's than through all of my many
sermons."

Reader 1: And only eternity will reveal the total number of
those whose lives have been dramatically changed by

God through the influence of this hymn from the pen of an invalid woman.

Reader 2: Though the message of "Just As I Am" is generally used as an invitation hymn for non-believers, it is also a reminder to Christians that our eternal standing with God is based solely on Christ's merits and not our own. Our daily sufficiency is found in these words of testimony by Charlotte Elliott—

Charlotte Elliott: "God sees, God guards, God guides me; His grace surrounds me and His voice continually bids me to be happy and holy in His service—just where I am!"

(Congregation sings "Just As I Am")

See page 146, *101 Hymn Stories*

- Indulgence says, "Drink your way out."
  Philosophy says, "Think your way out."
  Science says, "Invent your way out."
  Industry says, "Work your way out."
  Communism says, "Strike your way out."
  Militarism says, "Fight your way out."
  Christ says, "I AM THE WAY OUT."

  —Author unknown

Lead On, O King Eternal

3 Characters: 2 Readers, Ernest Shurtleff

Reader 1: One of life's joyous experiences is the exciting view of one of our loved ones walking across a stage in an academic cap and gown and receiving that long-awaited diploma, following a challenging address to the graduating class of _____.

The hymn "Lead On, O King Eternal" was written for just such an event by Ernest Shurtleff (SHIRT-leff) as he was about to be graduated from Andover Seminary.

Reader 2: Ernest's classmates at the seminary were aware of the poetic abilities of their colleague and approached him with this request shortly before graduation—

Reader 1: "Ernest, why don't you write our class poem? After all, you have already published two volumes of poetry. What's the use of having a distinguished author in this class if he cannot rise to the occasion and do his class the honor of writing a good poem just for them?"

Reader 2: The 26-year-old future Congregational minister pondered a moment . . .

Ernest Shurtleff: "I don't know whether to ask for congratulations or condolences. But what kind of poem do you want?"

Reader 1: "Not the usual kind of sentimental slush associated with graduations. We've had enough of that in high school and college."

Ernest Shurtleff: "Well, then, do you want a poem or a hymn?"

Reader 1: "Make it a hymn, and write it so we can all sing it to a familiar tune."

Ernest Shurtleff: "Then our graduation hymn must be a militant marching song. We've been spending days of preparation here at seminary. Now the day of march has come and we must go out to follow the leadership of the King of Kings, to conquer the world under His banner. Without the roll of drums or the clashing of swords, though, we can fight the good fight of faith, and with our deeds of love and mercy, subdue the kingdom of this world for the Kingdom of our Lord!"

Reader 1: "That's a great idea for our class hymn, Ernest, and if you could only make your lines match our favorite 'Lancashire' (LAN-ca-SHUR) tune . . ."

Ernest Shurtleff: "You mean the one that goes . . ."

(hums a line or instruments play a portion of "Lead On, O King Eternal")

Reader 1: "Yes, yes, that's it . . . then we'd have a great new hymn written especially for our graduation."

Reader 2: With these ideas ringing in his mind, Ernest Shurtleff went to his room and within a short time completed these words for the young ministers to sing at their commencement.

(Instruments play softly while words are read)

✳ ✳ ✳ ✳

Ernest Shurtleff:

1. "Lead on, O King Eternal, the day of march has come!
Henceforth in fields of conquest Thy tents shall be our home;
Through days of preparation Thy grace has made us strong,
And now, O King Eternal, we lift our battle song.

2. Lead on, O King Eternal, 'till sin's fierce war shall cease,
And holiness shall whisper the sweet Amen of peace;
For not with swords loud clashing, nor roll of stirring drums;
With deeds of love and mercy, the heavenly Kingdom comes.

3.   Lead on, O King Eternal, we follow, not with fears,
For gladness breaks like morning where'er Thy face
    appears;
The cross is lifted o'er us; we journey in its light;
The crown awaits the conquest—Lead on, O God of
    Might!"

✳ ✳ ✳ ✳

Reader 1:   Following his graduation from Andover Seminary, Ernest Shurtleff gave distinctive service in Congregational churches in California, Massahusetts and
Minnesota. During this time he was awarded the Doctor of Divinity degree from Ripon College in Wiscon-
sin in recognition of his outstanding pulpit ministries.

Reader 2:   In 1905, Dr. Shurtleff and his family moved to Europe, where he organized the American Church in
Frankfort, Germany. Later in Paris, France, he carried
on a remarkable ministry with students and became
widely known for his "deeds of love and mercy" with
the poor and needy of that city.

Reader 1:   At the age of 55, however, and at the very height of
his fruitful ministry in Paris, Ernest Shurtleff was called
to his heavenly home to receive the "crown that awaits
the conquest."

Reader 2:   The well-suited martial music for this text was written 52 years earlier by a noted English organist and
composer named Henry Smart. Originally Mr. Smart
composed this music for a missionary hymn text, "From
Greenland's Icy Mountains," to be used at a music fes-
tival in England observing the 300th anniversary of the
Reformation in that country.

(Instruments begin playing softly)

✳ ✳ ✳ ✳

Reader 1:   Although expressions such as "days of preparation," "fields of conquest," "thy tents shall be our home,"
were intended to challenge the 1887 graduating class of
Andover Seminary, the truths of this hymn can be applied to our personal lives today.

Reader 2: This is not the time for us to slacken our service for the Lord. May we earnestly live so that one day we may be able to say with the apostle Paul . . .

Reader 1: "I have fought the good fight, I have finished the race, I have kept the faith."

Reader 2: "Now there is in store for me the crown of righteousness, which the Lord, the righteous Judge, will award to me on that day—and not only to me, but also to all who have longed for His appearing" (2 Tim. 4:7, 8).

Ernest Shurtleff: "THE CROWN AWAITS THE CONQUEST—LEAD ON, O GOD OF MIGHT!"

* * * *

(Congregation sings "Lead On, O King Eternal")

See page 152, *101 Hymn Stories*

- "The world at its worst needs the church at its best."
  —Author unknown

- "God wants us to be victors, not victims; to grow, not grovel; to soar, not sink; to overcome, not to be overwhelmed."   —William H. Ward

- Let us recognize our inadequacy with Christ—our invincibility with Him."   —Author unknown

- "I will place no value on anything I have or may possess except in relation to the kingdom of Christ."
  —David Livingstone

- "I must lose myself in action, lest I wither in despair."   —Alfred Tennyson

My Country, 'Tis of Thee (America)

4 Characters: 2 Readers, Lowell Mason, Samuel Smith

Reader 1:   Music has always been closely allied with patriotism. Every country has nationalistic music that is distinctly its own. For a number of years, however, the United States lacked such patriotic songs. Even our national anthem, "The Star Spangled Banner," was not officially adopted as such until 1931.

Reader 2:   An earnest concern for a worthy hymn to represent our young nation prompted a 24-year-old theological student to complete the text for this hymn in less than 30 minutes.

(Instruments play a portion of "My Country, 'Tis of Thee")

Reader 2:   This well-loved patriotic hymn, "America" or "My Country, 'Tis of Thee," was written by Samuel Francis Smith in 1831.

Reader 1:   Samuel Smith was one of the outstanding Baptist preachers of America during the past century. He was born in 1808 in Boston, Massachusetts, where much of our country's history began.

Reader 2:   Samuel grew up under the sound of the chimes that could be heard from the Old North Church, and just up the road was Copps Hill Burying Ground. During the War of 1812, British soldiers had desecrated the graves of the early founders of the Massachusetts Bay Colony by placing cannons between the graves.

Reader 1:   The bitter impressions of that war remained with Samuel for many years. He spent much time studying epitaphs (EP-i-tafs) on the patriots' gravestones in the Copps Hill Burying Ground. He was a serious boy who seemed to prefer reading and writing poems to playing games with other children.

Reader 2:   At an early age Samuel Smith's unusual scholastic ability became evident. He enrolled at Harvard when just 17 years of age and later prepared for the ministry at

Andover Theological Seminary, the first institution in this country established solely for the training of clergymen. After he was ordained as a Baptist minister, Smith served various historic churches and during this time wrote several important books as well as 150 hymns.

Reader 1: While he was still in seminary, Smith was approached one day by his close friend, Lowell Mason, a noted music educator and church musician, who was the choirmaster at Park Street Congregational Church of Boston.

Lowell Mason: "Samuel, I have just received this book of German patriotic songs extolling the virtues of their land and asking God's continued blessing upon that nation. What a shame that we don't have a similar national hymn that would enable our American people to direct praise and thanks to God for this great land He has allowed us to enjoy."

Samuel Smith: "Do you mean, Dr. Mason, that no one throughout this vast country has ever written such a hymn for our people?"

Lowell Mason: "That's right, Samuel, we just do not have one. It has been my fervent prayer for some time now that God will guide some person soon to supply our nation with such a hymn.

By the way, since you are so fluent in German, would you be willing to translate several of these songs for me?"

Samuel Smith: "I agreed, but as I worked on these translations, I felt the impulse to write a patriotic song of my own, adapted to the familiar tune long associated with the English words of 'God Save the King.' Picking up a piece of scrap paper which lay near by, I wrote at once—probably within 30 minutes—the hymn 'America' as it is now known everywhere. The whole hymn stands today as it first appeared on that bit of scrap paper."

Reader 2: After completing the task of translating the book of German songs for his friend Lowell Mason, Smith returned the collection to him, not realizing that he had left the scrap of paper containing the verses of "America" inside the German book. Soon, however, Smith forgot about the patriotic verses he had written and misplaced.

Reader 1: On July 4th, 1831, Samuel Smith joined the huge crowd gathered at the corner of Tremont and Park Streets at Boston Common where the Independence Day service at Park Street Church was to be held outdoors. After Lowell Mason had directed several songs, a choir of 200 children, seated on the steps of the church, suddenly rose and began to sing with loud, clear voices—"MY COUNTRY, 'TIS OF THEE, SWEET LAND OF LIBERTY, OF THEE I SING . . ."

Samuel Smith: "I was astounded and could hardly believe what I heard—my verses, written so hurriedly five months earlier. I had actually forgotten ever having written them! Dr. Mason had never mentioned to me that he had found my scrap of paper and was going to use this occasion to introduce the new patriotic hymn."

Reader 1: Though the text of this hymn is distinctively American, the tune is an international one. It is the official or semi-official national melody of at least 20 countries, particularly that of England, where "God Save the King" has been sung for more than 200 years.

Reader 2: The origin of this tune seems to go back deeply into the singing traditions of Europe, where traces of it have been found in Swiss music as early as the seventeenth century. The tune has also been found in the musical heritage of such other countries as Germany, Sweden, and Russia, and it is perhaps the most adopted melody ever composed.

(Instruments begin playing softly)

✳   ✳   ✳   ✳

Reader 1: Samuel Smith's text was first published in 1832, in a musical journal edited by Lowell Mason. Now more than 150 years later, none of our national holidays would be complete without "America." As one writer stated—

Reader 2: "The hymn is so strong in simplicity and deep in its trust in God, children and philosophers can repeat the hymn together. Every crisis will hear it above the storm."

✳   ✳   ✳   ✳

(Congregation sings "My Country, 'Tis of Thee")

See page 161, *101 Hymn Stories*

My Faith Looks Up to Thee

4 Characters: 2 Readers, Ray Palmer, Dr. Lowell Mason

Reader 1: How do we as sinful people find favor with a holy God? The Scriptures clearly state that without a personal response of faith in Him it is impossible for us to please God—"because anyone who comes to Him must believe that He exists and that He rewards those who earnestly seek Him" (Hebrews 11:6).

Reader 2: "Therefore, since we have been justified through faith, we have peace with God through our Lord Jesus Christ" (Romans 5:1).

Reader 1: A lonely twenty-two-year-old school teacher who had experienced a discouraging year of illness and other difficulties lifted his eyes one evening in desperation to God and was led to write the thoughtful words of this beloved hymn—

(Instruments play one verse of "My Faith Looks Up to Thee")

Reader 1: "My Faith Looks Up to Thee," one of our finest hymns on the subject of personal faith, was written by Ray Palmer in the year 1832.

Reader 2: When just thirteen years of age, Palmer was forced to drop out of school and take a job as a clerk in Boston. He began attending the historic Park Street Congregational Church and there professed Christ as his Savior. Soon he felt the call of God to become a minister of the gospel. He resumed his education at Andover Academy and later was graduated from Yale University.

Reader 1: While at Yale, Ray Palmer took a part-time teaching position in a private girls' school in New York City. It was a difficult job that eventually affected his health and brought him to a state of depression.

Reader 2: One night while reading a German poem picturing a needy sinner kneeling before the cross, Ray Palmer was so moved that he translated the lines into English.

Immediately his mind was filled with the thoughts of "My Faith Looks Up to Thee."

Ray Palmer: "The words for these stanzas were born out of my own soul with very little effort. I recall that I wrote the verses with tender emotion. There was not the slightest thought of writing for another eye, least of all writing a hymn for Christian worship. It is well remembered that while writing the last line, 'Oh, bear me safe above, a ransomed soul,' the thought of the whole work of redemption and salvation was involved in those words, suggesting the theme of eternal praises, and this brought me to a degree of emotion that caused abundant tears."

Reader 1:   Mr. Palmer copied his verses into a small notebook and thought no more of them except to read them occasionally for his own devotions. Two years later, while walking down a busy street in Boston, he chanced to meet his friend, Dr. Lowell Mason, who was well-known in nineteenth century musical circles.

Dr. Lowell Mason: "Mr. Palmer, how good to see you again. I am just now in the process of compiling a new hymnal for our churches. I know that you like to write poetic verses and I was wondering if by any chance you might have some lines that would lend themselves to a new hymn?"

Ray Palmer: "I showed him the verses in my little notebook. We stepped into a store together, and a copy of the poem was made and given to him. Without much notice, he put it into his pocket. Several days later, however, when we met again in the street, he scarcely waited to greet me . . ."

Dr. Lowell Mason: "Mr. Palmer, you may live many years and do many good things, but I think you will be best known to posterity as the author of 'My Faith Looks Up to Thee.'"

Reader 2:   Lowell Mason had in the meantime composed a melody for this text, a tune which he called "Olivet," in reference to the hymn's message. The hymn in its present form appeared in print that same year in a hymnal edited by Mason. And from that time to the present, nearly every church hymnal has included these thoughtful and deeply devotional lines.

(Instruments begin playing softly)

* * * *

Reader 1:   And Dr. Lowell Mason's prediction about Palmer and his hymn certainly came true. Ray Palmer did accomplish much for God until his death at the age of 79. He became recognized as an outstanding evangelical minister and pastored two large Congregational churches in the East for 39 years.

Reader 2:   Palmer was the author of several popular volumes of religious verse and devotional essays. He also wrote 37 other fine hymns, for which he would never accept payment.

Reader 1:   Yet Dr. Palmer is best remembered today for his very first hymn text, a statement of personal faith in Christ written when he was just 22 years of age.

Reader 2:   May we also reaffirm our love and commitment to Christ as we sing these words of testimony: "My faith looks up to Thee, Thou Lamb of Calvary, Savior Divine!"

* * * *

(Congregation sings "My Faith Looks Up to Thee")

See page 189, *101 More Hymn Stories*

Drama 31

My Redeemer

5 Characters: 2 Readers, Philip P. Bliss,
Major Daniel Whittle, James McGranahan

Reader 1:   Many of our finest hymns were born out of some deeply moving experience, often a very tragic one. Our featured hymn for this service, though expressing a joyful note of praise, is associated with tragedy in the author's life.

(Instruments play a portion of "My Redeemer")

Reader 1:   This familiar gospel hymn, "I Will Sing of My Redeemer and His Wondrous Love to Me," was written by Philip P. Bliss in 1876.

Reader 2:   Philip Bliss was one of the most influential musicians in the growth of early gospel hymnody in this country. He was born in Clearfield County, Pennsylvania in 1838. As a child he lived in extreme poverty on a farm and later in a lumbering community.

Philip P. Bliss: "After I was converted at the age of twelve there in our poor lumbering community in Pennsylvania, where I was known as Philip, the large, awkward, overgrown Bliss boy, I developed a keen interest in sacred music. I composed my first song during the early teen years. My love for music eventually led to a career in teaching, writing and editing gospel songs for the George Root Music Company in Chicago. There my work came to the attention of evangelist D.L. Moody and his associate, Ira Sankey. Soon I was invited to join them in their evangelistic ministry. Often I sang solos, led the large congregations in singing, and assisted Mr. Sankey in publishing new gospel song books. Now that I'm in my mid-30's I still find much fulfillment in serving God in this way."

Reader 1:   In addition to being known as a man with a commanding stature and an impressive personality for leading congregational singing, Philip Bliss was highly regarded by his fellow music colleagues. George

Stebbins, also a noted gospel song writer of that time, once paid Bliss this tribute ...

Reader 2: "There has been no writer of verse since his time who has shown such a grasp of the fundamental truths of the gospel or such a gift for putting them into poetic and singable form."

Reader 1: And Dr. George Root, also an influential and outstanding music editor and composer, said of Bliss:

Reader 2: "If ever a man seemed fashioned by the Divine Hand for special and exalted work, that man was Philip P. Bliss."

Reader 1: Yet at the age of 38 when he had reached the very height of his fruitful music ministry, Bliss's life was suddenly ended in tragedy.

Reader 2: During the Christmas season of 1876, Bliss and his wife had visited his mother at his childhood home in Rome, Pennsylvania. As they were returning by train to Chicago to assist in an evangelistic campaign, a railroad bridge near Ashtabula, Ohio collapsed. Their train plunged into a ravine sixty feet below and caught fire. One hundred passengers perished!

Reader 1: Bliss somehow survived the fall and escaped through a window. However, as he frantically searched through the wreckage in an attempt to rescue his wife, he perished with her in the fire. Neither body was ever recovered!

Reader 2: Quite miraculously, however, among Bliss's belongings in the train wreckage was a manuscript on which Bliss evidently had been working. The hymn text he had just finished was "My Redeemer."

Reader 1: The shocking news of Bliss's fatal accident made a profound impact on evangelical Christians everywhere. Upon hearing of it, two of his personal friends, evangelist Major Daniel Whittle and musician James McGranahan, left separately for the site of the accident, each hoping to find some trace of their mutually esteemed friend.

Reader 2: Moving about in the large crowd, McGranahan recognized the Major, though they had never met. The Major, too, had heard from Bliss that James McGranahan was a very talented musician and should be in full-time Christian service. Major Whittle's first thought upon seeing young McGranahan was—"There stands the man Philip Bliss has chosen for his successor." The Major immediately approached him . . .

Major Whittle: "Mr. McGranahan, I've heard much about you and I believe that you are the man that God has chosen to continue the work that our dear friend Philip has begun."

Reader 1:   McGranahan took the manuscript of Bliss's hymn text that Major Whittle had located in a trunk and promised . . .

James McGranahan: "I will prayerfully attempt to compose the music for these words and I will also consider your personal challenge to commit my life to a full-time ministry with you in the work of evangelism."

Reader 1:   They returned to Chicago together and spent much time talking and praying about this matter. Soon James McGranahan made his decision to use his musical ability for God's service alone. For the next eleven years these two talented men shared a very fruitful ministry. They traveled extensively in evangelistic work and collaborated in a great number of fine gospel songs which have been widely used.

Reader 2:   At their first public rally together following the accident when the hymn "My Redeemer" was introduced, the large Chicago audience was told that Major Whittle had found the text among Bliss' belongings and James McGranahan had just recently composed the music for the words.

(Instruments begin playing softly)

❋   ❋   ❋   ❋

One can imagine the enthusiasm that accompanied the singing at that service. We share in their inspiration as we sing these final words written by Philip P. Bliss—

Philip P. Bliss: "I will sing of my Redeemer and His heav'nly love to me; He from death to life hath brought me, Son of God with Him to be."

❋   ❋   ❋   ❋

(Congregation sings "My Redeemer")

See page 164, *101 Hymn Stories*

Near to the Heart of God

3 Characters: 2 Readers, Rev. Cleland McAfee

Reader 1: An effective hymn can be defined as "a spiritual expression that is born in the soul of one individual and in turn ministers to the heartfelt needs of others." The devotional hymn "Near to the Heart of God" is an excellent example of that truth. It was written in 1901 by a Presbyterian minister, Cleland McAfee, after receiving the tragic news that diphtheria had just claimed the lives of his two beloved nieces.

Reader 2: Stunned and shocked, Pastor McAfee turned to God and the Scriptures. Soon these words and the music began to flow from his grieving heart—

(Instruments play "Near to the Heart of God"
softly while the words are read)

❋ ❋ ❋ ❋

Rev. McAfee: 1. "There is a place of quiet rest, near to the heart of God,

A place where sin cannot molest, near to the heart of God.

2. There is a place of comfort sweet, near to the heart of God,

A place where we our Savior meet, near to the heart of God.

3. There is a place of full release, near to the heart of God,

A place where all is joy and peace, near to the heart of God.

O Jesus, blest Redeemer, sent from the heart of God,

Hold us who wait before Thee, near to the heart of God."

❋ ❋ ❋ ❋

Reader 2:   Several days later during the time of the double funeral, Rev. McAfee sang the new hymn for his bereaved brother and sister-in-law, parents of the two girls.

Reader 1:   The following Sunday, Dr. McAfee's church choir repeated their pastor's new song as a communion hymn at the worship service.

Reader 2:   Another brother, also a Presbyterian minister, was so impressed with the simple but comforting message of this hymn that he carried it back to his pastorate in Berkeley, California. "Near to the Heart of God" soon became widely used to minister comfort and spiritual healing to God's people everywhere.

Reader 1:   Following two successful pastorates at the First Presbyterian Church of Chicago and Lafayette Presbyterian Church in Brooklyn, New York, for the next eighteen years Cleland McAfee served as a professor of systematic theology at the McCormick Seminary in Chicago.

Reader 2:   During his retirement years in New Hampshire, he remained active and became widely known as an eminent theologian, a brilliant speaker, and the author of numerous books and scholarly papers.

Reader 1:   Dr. McAfee was honored by his denomination by being elected moderator of the General Assembly of the Presbyterian Church.

Reader 2:   Yet today Dr. Cleland McAfee is no doubt best remembered for this tender devotional hymn, written during a time of deep personal sorrow.

(Instruments begin playing softly and continue to the end)

✳   ✳   ✳   ✳

Reader 1:   The hymnal can be a source of much comfort when we are facing a very difficult situation. It is thrilling to realize how Christians through the centuries have responded to God, to share in the spiritual expressions of others, and to sense the emotional and physical struggles that prompted our enduring hymns to be born. But then, above all, when we open God's Word itself we find His eternal promises and further help for our daily needs.

Reader 2:   "The Lord is close to the brokenhearted and saves those who are crushed in spirit." "When anxiety was great within me, Your comfort brought joy to my spirit" (Psalm 34:18; 94:19).

Reader 1:   But God does not provide comfort for us in our need merely that we might remain comfortable; rather He desires that we in turn might learn to comfort and encourage others in their times of stress . . . "to provide for those who grieve a garment of praise instead of a spirit of despair" (Isaiah 61:3).

Reader 2:   "Praise be to the God and Father of compassion and the God of all comfort, who comforts us in all our troubles, so that we can comfort those in any trouble with the comfort we ourselves have received from God" (2 Corinthians 1:3,4).

Reader 1:   We can be a healing balm to those around us whose lives are broken and grieving. The singing of this hymn should also remind each of us of the necessity of relying upon our God and His Holy Word more completely each day, as did Dr. McAfee in his time of need—

Reader 2:   "Hold us who wait before Thee, near to the heart of God."

✳ ✳ ✳ ✳

(Congregation sings "Near to the Heart of God")

See page 197, *101 More Hymn Stories*

Now Thank We All Our God

4 Characters: 2 Readers, Swedish Commander,
Pastor Martin Rinkart

Reader 1:   Upon hearing the majestic hymn featured today, one would never realize that this outburst of gratitude was written during times of great tragedy. As a result of some of the most severe human suffering imaginable during the European Thirty Years' War of 1618-1648—a war that has been described as one of the most devastating in history—this stately hymn of the church was born. And still today we sing this noble expression of praise with great fervor, especially during each Thanksgiving season.

(Instruments play one stanza of "Now Thank We All Our God")

Reader 2:   "Now Thank We All Our God" has been used more widely in German churches than any other hymn, with the exception of Martin Luther's "A Mighty Fortress Is Our God." The text was written by a German Lutheran pastor, Martin Rinkart, shortly before the close of the Thirty Years' War.

Reader 1:   Martin Rinkart was born in 1586, in the province of Saxony, Germany. He was the son of a poor coppersmith, and as a boy served as a chorister in the famous St. Thomas Church in Leipzig, (LIPE-zig) Germany, where the renowned Johann Sebastian Bach (BAHK) was later music director. Rinkart worked his way through the University of Leipzig and was ordained to the ministry of the state Lutheran church. At the age of thirty-one he was called to be a pastor in his native town of Eilenberg (I-len-BERG). He arrived just when the dreadful bloodshed of the Thirty Years' War was beginning, and spent the remaining thirty-two years of his life faithfully ministering to the needy people of this community.

Reader 2:   Because Eilenberg was a walled city, it became a frightfully over-crowded refuge for numerous political and military fugitives. Throughout the war years several waves of deadly disease and famine swept the city as various armies marched through, leaving death and destruction behind.

Reader 1:   Though Martin Rinkart often had difficulty in providing adequate food and clothing even for his own immediate family, his home became a refuge for afflicted people.

Reader 2:   The plague of 1637 was particularly severe. At its height Rinkart was the only minister remaining to care for the sick and dying. He conducted as many as 40 to 50 funeral services daily, often assisting in the actual digging of the graves. Most of his own family members died during this time.

Reader 1:   Yet, amazingly, in spite of all his pastoral responsibilities and difficulties, Rinkart was a prolific writer as well as a musician. He wrote sixty-six hymns and seven dramatic productions based on the events of the Protestant Reformation.

Reader 2:   During the closing years of the war, the city of Eilenberg was overrun by invading armies at least three times—once by the Austrian Army and twice by the Swedes. During one of the occupations by the Swedish Army, the commander sent this message to Pastor Rinkart—

Swedish Commander: "Our Swedish Army demands from your people the sum of money stated below."

Pastor Martin Rinkart: "But, sir, my people are already impoverished and simply unable to meet this demand! Could not the unreasonable amount of this levy be lowered?"

Swedish Commander: "Under no circumstances will the amount be decreased. Your people must either meet our demand or they will all be killed."

Pastor Martin Rinkart: "My humble parishioners, our request has been denied. Come, my children, we can find no mercy with this man; let us take refuge with God."

Reader 2:   On his knees Rinkart led his parishoners in prayer and in the singing of a familiar hymn. This demonstration of spiritual fervency so moved the Swedish commander that he lowered the demands of tribute, making it possible for the poor people of Eilenberg to pay and survive.

Reader 1:   The fine English translation of this German text was made by Catherine Winkworth more than 200 years after it was written by Pastor Rinkart. The hymn has since been widely used in English-speaking churches.

Reader 2:   The stirring music for this text was written by one of Germany's finest and most prolific seventeenth century composers, Johann Crüger (CROO-ger). Shortly after it had been composed, Rinkart's text wedded with Crüger's tune appeared in a popular German hymnal published by Crüger. And since that time few hymnals have been published anywhere that have not included this inspiring hymn.

Reader 1:   Despite the pressures and hardships of his life, Rinkart continued to minister God's love to his people until he was called to his heavenly home at the age of 63.

(Instruments begin playing softly)

✳   ✳   ✳   ✳

Reader 2:   Pastor Martin Rinkart's triumphant personal expressions of gratitude and trust contained in his hymn reaffirm this thrilling scriptural truth—

Reader 1:   "Who shall separate us from the love of Christ? Shall trouble or hardship or persecution or famine or nakedness or danger or sword?"

Reader 2:   "No, in all these things we are more than conquerors through Him who loved us" (Romans 8:35, 37).

✳   ✳   ✳   ✳

(Congregation sings "Now Thank We All Our God")

See page 172, *101 Hymn Stories*

O for a Thousand Tongues

3 Characters: 2 Readers, Charles Wesley

(Instruments begin by playing one verse of "O for a Thousand Tongues"—"Azmon" Tune)

Reader 1: Even though the many years of tedious psalm-singing had been earlier improved by the free verse wording of Isaac Watts, the eighteenth century church was truly ready for another important musical change.

Reader 2: God providentially raised up Charles Wesley with his warm experiential hymns like "O for a Thousand Tongues" so that the church's song was kept alive and vibrant.

Charles Wesley: "Shortly after my older brother John and I had been graduated from Oxford University, where we were first called 'Methodists' because of our methodical habits of living and studying, we were ordained by the Church of England and sent to America to help stabilize the rough colonists in Georgia with religious services and to evangelize the Indians. Crossing the Atlantic, we came into contact with a group of German Moravian Christians on our boat. We had previously heard about these people—their spiritual warmth, missionary zeal, and especially about their enthusiastic hymn-singing. We were both much impressed by them, especially during a raging storm when it was evident that they were the only passengers aboard ship who were able to maintain their composure in the face of imminent danger. John wrote the following entry in his diary of January 25th, 1736—"

Reader 1: "In the midst of the reading of the Psalm wherewith their service began, the sea broke over, split the mainsail, covered the ship and poured in between the decks. A terrible screaming began among the English passengers. But the German Moravians looked up and, without intermission, calmly sang on. I asked one of them afterwards, 'Were you not afraid?' He answered, 'Thank God, No!'"

Reader 2:   Following a brief discouraging time in America, John and Charles Wesley returned to England, where they attended a meeting in the Aldersgate Hall in London with a group of devout Moravians. Through their influence, the Wesley brothers began to realize that though they had been zealously involved in Christian service, neither had ever personally experienced God's real love and joy. In May, 1738, both John and Charles had a spiritually "heart-warming" experience. From that time on, their ministries took on a new dimension of spiritual power.

Reader 1:   Both brothers ministered with an indomitable spirit, usually working 15 to 18 hours each day. It is estimated that they traveled a quarter of a million miles throughout Great Britain, mostly on horseback, while conducting more than 40,000 public services. They never tired of telling individuals of all social classes the simple message of God's mercy and the good news that any life could be changed dramatically simply by accepting and believing the truths of the gospel.

Reader 2:   To enhance this ministry, Charles wrote more than 6,500 hymn texts. Hardly a day passed without the suggestion of some new verses. It was his earnest concern when writing these texts that "sinners would be aroused, saints encouraged, and that all would be educated in the mysteries of the Christian faith."

Charles Wesley: "In 1749 on the 11th anniversary of my own 'heart-warming' experience at Aldersgate, I was inspired by a chance remark of an influential Moravian leader and friend named Peter Bohler (BOH-ler). Expressing his spiritual joy he exclaimed, 'O Brother Wesley, the Lord has done so much for my life. Had I a thousand tongues, I would praise Christ Jesus with every one of them.' Immediately words of praise began to flow from my own heart in gratitude for all that the great Redeemer had done in providing my salvation and spiritual joy.

Reader 1:   The text for "O for a Thousand Tongues" originally had 19 stanzas and when published was titled, "For the Anniversary of One's Conversion." Many of the verses which are no longer used dealt directly with Charles Wesley's own personal experience—

Reader 2:   "I felt my Lord's atoning blood close to my soul applied:

Me, me He loved—the Son of God for me, for me He died."

(Instruments begin playing softly)

* * * *

Reader 1:   But the stanzas that remain in nearly every church hymnal have provided God's people with an inspiring hymn of praise, voicing with the saints of the ages majestic worship to our eternal God.

Reader 2:   "Glory to God and praise and love be ever, ever giv'n by saints below and saints above—the Church in earth and heav'n."

* * * *

(Congregation sings "O for a Thousand Tongues")

See page 180, *101 Hymn Stories*

- "Praise is the dress of saints in heaven— it is only reasonable that they should begin wearing it here below."   —Charles H. Spurgeon

- "Christianity is not a theory or speculation, but a life; not a philosophy of life, but a living presence. This realization can turn any gloom into a song."
—Samuel Taylor Coleridge

O God, Our Help in Ages Past

2 Characters: 2 Readers

Reader 1: "Lord, You have been our dwelling place throughout all generations. Before the mountains were born or You brought forth the earth and the world, from everlasting to everlasting You are God" (Psalm 90:1, 2).

Reader 2: The featured hymn for our service today is a paraphrase of Psalm 90.

(Instruments play one stanza of "O God, Our Help in Ages Past")

Reader 1: This stirring hymn of worship, "O God, Our Help in Ages Past," was written more than 250 years ago by Isaac Watts, a young English minister who has become known as "the father of the English hymn." He is credited with laying the foundations for our present-day congregational singing.

Reader 2: Psalm 90's theme is a commentary on the subject of time.

Reader 1: "For a thousand years in Your sight are like a day that has just gone by, or like a watch in the night" (Psalm 90:4).

Reader 2: "The length of our days is seventy years—or eighty, if we have the strength; yet their span is but trouble and sorrow, for they quickly pass, and we fly away" (Psalm 90:10).

Reader 1: "Teach us to number our days aright, that we may gain a heart of wisdom. Satisfy us in the morning with Your unfailing love, that we may sing for joy and be glad all our days" (Psalm 90:12, 14).

Reader 2: "Establish the work of our hands for us—

Together: Yes, establish the work of our hands" (Psalm 90:17).

Reader 1: Isaac Watts' paraphrasing of Scripture was a bold departure for his time. The music of the church had become the strict and unaccompanied singing of ponderous metrical psalms. To have used your own words and thoughts for a text would have been considered an insult to God. It was believed that only the literal words of Scripture were worthy of being sung.

Reader 2: At an early age Watts became deeply concerned with the deplorable state to which congregational singing had degenerated in most English-speaking churches. His father one day challenged him—

Reader 1: "Isaac, if you're so unhappy with the congregational singing in this church, why don't you write something better for us to sing?"

Reader 2: "I intend to do just that, Father. I'm going to re-word the psalms by Christianizing them with a New Testament message and style that will make them easier to sing and more spiritually uplifting."

Reader 1: For the next two years Isaac Watts wrote a new hymn text each week for the Congregational church worshippers in Southampton, England. Then in 1719, at the early age of 25, Watts published an important hymnal titled *The Psalms of David Imitated in the Language of the New Testament,* paraphrasing nearly the entire psalter into Christian verse. In addition to "O God, Our Help in Ages Past," several of his other hymn texts still widely sung today include such favorites as—

Reader 2: "Joy to the World," a paraphrase of Psalm 98; "Jesus Shall Reign," a version of Psalm 72; and "Before Jehovah's Awful Throne," based on Psalm 100.

Reader 1: As time passed, Watts grew more convinced that writers should express praise and devotion to God freely in their own words rather than being limited to the literal words of Scripture. These hymn settings became known as "hymns of human composure" and include these favorites—

Reader 2: "When I Survey the Wondrous Cross," "Am I a Soldier of the Cross?" and "I Sing the Mighty Pow'r of God." Watts also wrote the first collection of hymns especially for children.

Reader 1: Throughout his lifetime Isaac Watts wrote more than 600 hymns. Because of his bold departure from the traditional psalms of that time and his writing of "human composure hymns," Watts was generally considered a radical churchman in his day. But now, more than two and one half centuries later, his memory and hymns are highly revered by Christians everywhere.

Reader 2:   A great hymn text deserves majestic music. No one has ever disputed the musical worth of this hymn's "St. Anne" tune, composed by William Croft in 1708. Croft was recognized as one of the finest English church musicians of his time. He was the organist at the Church of St. Anne in London during the reign of Queen Anne. The tune was dedicated to her.

(Instruments begin playing softly)

*   *   *   *

Reader 1:   Through the earnest efforts of a young preacher and writer named Isaac Watts, who desired to set the 90th psalm into New Testament language, combined with the skill of a talented church musician, William Croft, a classic hymn was born that holds an enduring place in Christian worship.

Reader 2:   As we face the uncertainties of each tomorrow, may we do so with the confidence that the God of "ages past" is still "our hope for years to come." The One who has faithfully directed our lives to this very moment is truly worthy of our complete trust for all the days ahead.

*   *   *   *

(Congregation sings "O God, Our Help in Ages Past")

See page 183, *101 Hymn Stories*

O Little Town of Bethlehem

3 Characters: 2 Readers, Phillips Brooks

Reader 1:   "But you, Bethlehem, though you are small among the clans of Judah, out of you will come for Me One who will be ruler over Israel" (Micah 5:2).

Reader 2:   What would Christmas be without its glorious music? Could you possibly imagine going through another season without hearing or singing this lovely carol?

(Instruments play a portion of "O Little Town of Bethlehem")

Reader 2:   "O Little Town of Bethlehem" was written by one of America's outstanding preachers of the past century, Phillips Brooks.

Phillips Brooks: "I wrote the words for 'O Little Town of Bethlehem' after returning from a trip to the Holy Land. The vivid remembrances of this experience—the feelings I recalled as I approached the city of Bethlehem on horseback, the awe of worshiping the Christ-child on Christmas Eve in the Church of the Nativity, said to be the place of our Lord's birth—all of this made an indelible impression upon my life."

Reader 1:   Brooks desired to communicate to the congregation of the Holy Trinity Church in Philadelphia his profound love for the Holy Land. Three years after his visit, while searching for a new Christmas carol for the children to sing at their annual Sunday school program, the still vivid memories of his Holy Land trip inspired the pastor to pen these descriptive words—

Phillips Brooks: "O little town of Bethlehem, how still we see thee lie! Above thy deep and dreamless sleep the silent stars go by; yet in thy dark streets shineth the everlasting light—the hopes and fears of all the years are met in thee tonight."

Reader 2:   Soon Brooks completed all four stanzas and met with his church organist, Lewis Redner, to plan the

Sunday school program. Brooks showed Redner his newly written poem.

Phillips Brooks: "Lewis, I'm going to make you responsible for composing a singable melody for these lines so that our children can sing them for this year's Christmas program."

Reader 1: Lewis Redner struggled for several weeks to write an appropriate tune for his pastor's new poem, but nothing ever seemed just right.

Reader 2: Then on the Saturday evening before the Sunday school program was to be given, Redner suddenly awakened from his sleep and quickly composed the present melody. He always insisted that the music was a gift from God.

Reader 1: In the next morning's Sunday school session Redner worked frantically to teach the children their new Christmas song for that evening. The carol was an immediate favorite with the boys and girls as it has been with children and adults everywhere to the present time.

Reader 2: "O Little Town of Bethlehem" was first published in 1874, six years after it was written. Although Brooks wrote a number of other Christmas and Easter carols for children, this is the only one to survive.

Reader 1: Phillips Brooks was born in Boston, Massachusetts, in 1835, and after graduation from Harvard University and the Episcopal Theological Seminary in Virginia at the age of 24, he began a long and distinguished career in the Episcopalian ministry. He served as pastor in Philadelphia for ten years and another ten years at the prestigious Trinity Church in Boston.

Reader 2: Phillips Brooks was often referred to as the "Prince of the Pulpit." His many published volumes of sermons have since become classics of American literature. He is said to have won the hearts of people with his preaching and writing as few clergymen have ever done. Soon after he was appointed to be bishop of all the Episcopalian churches throughout Massachusetts, his sudden and unexpected death at the age of 58 was greatly mourned by all.

Reader 1: Brooks was known as an impressive and gifted man—a giant in body, standing 6'6" tall, as well as a giant in heart and mind. His forceful yet eloquent preaching did much to combat the Unitarian movement rampant throughout New England during that time.

Reader 2: Though a bachelor throughout his life, Phillips Brooks was especially fond of children. It is said that he always kept a supply of toys, dolls and other objects of interest in his office so that youngsters would be encouraged to drop in and chat with him. A familiar sight was this impressive man of the pulpit sitting on the floor of his study sharing a time of fun with a group of girls and boys.

Reader 1: A five-year old girl was unusually upset when she hadn't seen her preacher friend for several Sundays. When told by her mother that God had taken their bishop to heaven, the child exclaimed—

Reader 2: "Oh, momma, how happy the angels must be!"

(Congregation sings "O Little Town of Bethlehem")

See page 186, *101 Hymn Stories*

• "O God our loving Father, help us rightly to remember the birth of Jesus . . . that we may share in the song of the angels, the gladness of the shepherds, and the worship of the wise men.

Close the door of hate and open the door of love all over the world. Deliver us from evil by the blessing that Christ brings, and teach us to be merry with clear hearts.

May the Christmas morning make us happy to be Thy children and the Christmas evening bring us to our beds with grateful thoughts, forgiving and forgiven, for Jesus' sake." Amen.

—Robert Louis Stevenson

Drama 37

Peace, Perfect Peace

3 Characters: 3 Readers

Reader 1: The quest for inner peace has been a universal struggle throughout the ages. A joyous, untroubled mind is one of life's greatest goals. Many seek it in money, success, pleasure and drugs—but all such pursuits end in failure and frustration.

Reader 2: True contentment has been described as that inner strength that enables us to live in daily calmness with the ability to face any of life's challenges.

Reader 1: The secret of this serenity, however, is not dependent upon our material possessions or achievements, but rather upon a tranquility that comes from the provisions of grace made available to us by our Heavenly Father.

Reader 2: God's gift of grace includes not only pardon from sin, deliverance from hell and the assurance of heaven but also provides all that we need to live abundant lives of peace and rest (John 10:10).

(Instruments play one stanza of "Peace, Perfect Peace")

Reader 3: Our featured hymn for this service, "Peace, Perfect Peace," reminds us that real peace is found only in a personal relationship with Christ.—"He Himself is our peace" (Ephesians 2:14).

This hymn text was written in 1875 by Edward Bickersteth, an English minister and bishop of the Anglican church.

Reader 1: Throughout his ministry Bishop Bickersteth was known as a strong and influential evangelical leader. He was also regarded highly for his many books of sermons, poetry and hymns.

Reader 2: While vacationing, Bickersteth visited a village parish church and was much impressed by the local minister's sermon based on this biblical text in Isaiah 26:3—

Reader 3: "Thou wilt keep him in perfect peace, whose mind is stayed on Thee, because he trusteth in Thee."

Reader 1: The pastor explained that the original Hebrew version of this verse reads—"Thou wilt keep him in *peace peace* whose mind is stayed on Thee . . ." The point of the sermon was that in repetition the Hebrew language conveyed the idea of absolute perfection.

Reader 2: That afternoon Bishop Bickersteth paid a call upon a dying relative in the area. He found the man in a deeply depressed and disturbed state of mind. Desiring to be of spiritual help, Bickersteth took his Bible and began reading and discussing the Scripture text from Isaiah that was still fresh in his mind from the morning's sermon.

Reader 1: Then taking a sheet of paper from a nearby desk, Bishop Bickersteth quickly wrote these comforting lines and read them to the dying man—

Reader 3:

1. Peace, perfect peace—in this dark world of sin? The blood of Jesus whispers peace within.

2. Peace, perfect peace—by thronging duties pressed? To do the will of Jesus, this is rest.

3. Peace, perfect peace—with sorrows surging round? On Jesus' bosom naught but calm is found.

4. Peace perfect peace—with loved ones far away? In Jesus' keeping we are safe, and they.

5. Peace, perfect peace—our future all unknown? Jesus we know, and He is on the throne.

Reader 2: The simply stated poem gave assurance to the dying relative as he slipped into eternity. These words still speak to us today.

Reader 1: From the Hebrew expression of *"peace peace"* comes the beginning phrase of each stanza—"Peace, perfect peace." Then five challenging questions are posed—

Reader 2: For each of these probing questions and difficult situations of life, Edward Bickersteth provided a straightforward spiritual answer, concluding with this forceful reminder—

Reader 3: "JESUS WE KNOW, AND HE IS ON THE THRONE!"
Reader 2: And it was Jesus Himself who left us this promise—
Reader 3: "In Me you may have peace. In this world you will
have trouble. But take heart! I have overcome the world"
(John 16:33).

(Instruments begin playing softly)

*　*　*　*

Reader 1: May the singing of this thoughtful hymn encourage us to appropriate God's grace more fully each day
and to experience His perfect peace in every circumstance of our lives.

*　*　*　*

*(Congregation sings "Peace, Perfect Peace." Sing the hymn
antiphonally—one section or group asking the question while another
group responds with the second line's affirmative answer.)*

See page 206, *101 Hymn Stories*

- "The more clearly we see the sovereignty of God, the
less perplexed we are by the calamities of man."
—Author unknown

- "The beginning of anxiety is the end of faith, and the
beginning of true faith is the end of anxiety."
—George Müeller

- "God whispers in our pleasures, but shouts in our
pain!"   —C.S. Lewis

Precious Lord, Take My Hand

3 Characters: 2 Readers, Thomas A. Dorsey

Reader 1:   "Let the word of Christ dwell in you richly as you teach and encourage one another with all wisdom, and as you sing psalms, hymns and spiritual songs with gratitude in your hearts to God" (Colossians 3:16).

Reader 2:   What did the apostle Paul mean in Ephesians 5:19 and again in Colossians 3:16 when he gave this instruction to the first century Christians living in Asia Minor—to sing "psalms, hymns and spiritual songs"? The psalms, no doubt, refer to the rich heritage of Jewish music of that time from the book of Psalms and other Old Testament Scripture, directing man's worship to the greatness and majesty of God the Father.

Reader 1:   The reference to hymns was an encouragement for those early believers to also sing musical expressions that were more concerned with New Testament truths and doctrines regarding the person and redemptive work of Christ.

Reader 2:   But to give a proper balance to their worship, the apostle wisely suggested the use of spiritual or experiential songs—those more spontaneous expressions that flow from one's innermost being out of a very personal love relationship with the Lord as prompted by the ministry of the Holy Spirit.

Reader 1:   We are featuring in this service one of these very intimate spiritual expressions—

(Instruments play a portion of "Precious Lord, Take My Hand")

Reader 2:   "Precious Lord, Take My Hand" has been a favorite with many since it was first written in the summer of 1932 by a black gospel musician, Thomas A. Dorsey.

Thomas A. Dorsey: "I was born in the year 1899. I grew up in a Christian home in Georgia. My father was an itinerant preacher and my mother played the pump organ in church. By the time I was ten or twelve, I had learned to play that organ too. As a preacher's kid, I was exposed to quite a bit of religious activity, and maybe that got into me some way, but I didn't follow it."

Reader 1:   Soon Thomas Dorsey became interested in jazz music. During the first World War he began composing songs for blues singers, achieving considerable fame and financial success.

Thomas A. Dorsey: "I put a band together and traveled around quite a bit. I guess I wrote over 150 blues songs, and some are popular yet. When we visited Europe a few years ago, I heard them still being played in Rome."

Reader 2:   But Thomas Dorsey could never forget the influence of his early religious training nor the memory of his godly parents. Even when busily playing in bars and clubs around the country, he still thought a great deal about his early life. In spite of many harrowing experiences and brushes with death, God always spared his life. Then as a young man in his twenties, Dorsey began to reflect seriously about himself: how God had preserved him on so many occasions and that he was now foolishly wasting his time and talents.

Thomas A. Dorsey: "It was in 1924 that I started to come back to God. I knew I was ruining my life. That year I wrote 'If I Don't Get There,' a gospel song that is still in the song books. Today I can say that all that I am, and all that I ever will be, all that I have, all that I will ever possess, I owe to God. He brought me out of sin."

Reader 1:   For the next few years, Thomas Dorsey was actively involved in singing for church services and writing gospel songs. But one day while ministering in a revival meeting in St. Louis, Missouri, he received a telegram informing him that his wife Nettie has just died suddenly while delivering their first child. Arriving home in South Chicago that same night, he was met with the further news that his infant son had also died. Both were buried in the same casket. The sorrow was more than Dorsey could bear.

Thomas A. Dorsey: "That was double trouble, and I couldn't take it. I said, 'God, You aren't worth a dime to me right now.' I felt as if He had treated me wrong. A few weeks later I was sitting with a friend, Theodore Frye, the gospel singer, trying to get over my grief. As I fingered the keyboard of a piano, I picked up a tune, which wasn't so original—but the words were. I called it 'Blessed Lord.' After I had gone over it and over it, I said, 'Come here, Frye. How do you like this song?' And I went over it again for him."

Reader 2:   Theodore Frye responded, "Well, the words are good, but the 'Blessed Lord' won't work. Why not call Him 'Precious Lord'?"

Thomas A. Dorsey: "'That does sound better,' I said. 'Let's go over it once more.' The next Sunday morning Frye's choir sang it at the Ebenezer Baptist Church, and I played the accompaniment. It tore up the church."

Reader 1:   Until the time of his death in 1965, Thomas Dorsey wrote approximately 250 gospel songs, including another popular spiritual, "Peace in the Valley." All of his songs were written with much conviction—

Thomas A. Dorsey: "My business is to try to bring people to Christ instead of leaving them where they are. I write all of my songs with a message. If there is no message, there is no need for having a song. I don't write for races, I don't write for colors. I write for all of God's people. I want them all to use it. I want the blessing to go to everybody. All people are my people. What I share with people is love, that is, the power of love. I try to lift their spirits and let them know that God still loves them. I want them to understand that God is still in business. He's still saving, and He can still give that power."

Reader 2:   Thomas Dorsey also had these instructions for enjoying gospel music—

Thomas A. Dorsey: "To listen to a gospel song properly, you've got to be in the mood. You have to give God your whole intelligence, your whole heart, your whole feeling. You have to be able to bring yourself inside the realm of this expression that is being handed out, so it will reach you."

(Instruments begin playing softly)

✳   ✳   ✳   ✳

Reader 1:   Yes, spiritual songs like "Precious Lord, Take My Hand" are born in the heart of one believer, often out of much adversity, and then they minister to the heartfelt needs of countless others who may be sharing a similar experience. That is why the apostle Paul instructed the early churches that they were to sing spiritual songs to one another as an important source of learning and encouragement.

Reader 2:   May each of us apply the lesson from this simple gospel song by Thomas Dorsey. Placing our hand in the hand of omnipotence, we trust our Heavenly Father implicitly as He tenderly guides us through this life. We joyfully anticipate that day when He welcomes us to our eternal home.

✳   ✳   ✳   ✳

(Congregation sings "Precious Lord, Take My Hand")

Not found in *101* or *101 More Hymn Stories*
See page 260 in *Amazing Grace*

Rescue the Perishing

4 Characters: 2 Readers, Fanny Crosby, Army Captain

Reader 1:   For more than 100 years gospel songs have been one of the important influences in directing individuals to a personal relationship with Christ. The genius of this early American music is its directness and simplicity—its almost artless rhyming and often childlike music. Gospel music has always been the music of and for the people. And the person who wrote and supplied the church with more gospel songs than any other writer was the blind American poetess, Fanny Jane Crosby.

Reader 2:   In her day Fanny Crosby was considered by many to be the greatest hymnwriter in America. As Johann Strauss reigned in Vienna as the "Waltz King" and John Philip Sousa in Washington as the "March King," Fanny Crosby was recognized in the latter nineteenth and early twentieth century as the "Hymn Queen." She wrote more than 8,000 gospel hymn texts before her death in 1915 at the age of 95.

Reader 1:   One reporter of that time summarized Fanny's reputation—

Reader 2:   "Everybody knows the name of Fanny Crosby. It is a question whether any name in the religious annals of America is better known. Who is there that has not heard and sung 'Rescue the Perishing,' 'Blessed Assurance,' 'He Hideth My Soul,' 'Draw Me Nearer,' 'Safe in the Arms of Jesus,' or 'Saved by Grace'? In far-off mission stations, down in the dark unlovely underworld of cities, in homes, churches, and camps—these hymns have brought solace and encouragement to millions. They are songs that will never die."

Reader 1:   It is always difficult to single out one particular Fanny Crosby favorite. But we are opening our hymnals to one that reminds us pointedly of our Christian responsibility—that of evangelizing people who desperately need to hear the good news of the gospel.

(Instruments play a portion of "Rescue the Perishing")

Reader 2:   This well-known gospel hymn, "Rescue the Perishing," was written by Fanny Crosby in 1869.

Fanny Crosby: "Like many of my hymns, it was written following a personal experience at the New York City Mission. I usually tried to get to the mission at least one night a week to talk to 'my boys.' I was addressing a large company of working men one hot summer evening, when the thought kept forcing itself on my mind that some mother's boy must be rescued that night or he might be eternally lost. So I made a pressing plea that if there was a boy present who had wandered from his mother's home and teaching, he should come to me at the end of the service. A young man of eighteen came forward—"

Reader 2:   "Did you mean me, Miss Crosby? I promised my mother to meet her in heaven, but as I am now living, that will be impossible."

Fanny Crosby: "We prayed for him and suddenly he arose with a new light in his eyes."

Reader 2:   "Now I am ready to meet my mother in heaven, for I have found God."

Fanny Crosby: "A few days before, Mr. Doane, the composer, had sent me a tune for a new song to be titled 'Rescue the Perishing,' based on Luke 14:23. During this time I had been thinking and praying earnestly about this text: 'Go out into the highways and hedges, and compel them to come in, that my house may be filled.' While I sat in the Bowery Mission that evening, the line came to me— 'rescue the perishing, care for the dying.' I could think of nothing else. When I arrived home following the service, I went to work on that hymn at once, and before I retired it was ready for Mr. Doane's melody."

Reader 1:   William Doane was a close personal friend of Fanny Crosby and collaborated with her on many of her hymn texts. Though he was a successful businessman, Doane was also known as one of the leading gospel musicians of that era, writing more than 2,000 texts and tunes.

Reader 2: "Rescue the Perishing," like so many of Fanny Crosby's soul-stirring songs, has been influential in bringing conviction and repentance to many. Ira Sankey, who used this hymn often in his evangelistic crusades with Mr. Moody, told this story—

Reader 1: On a stormy night a middle-aged man staggered into the New York Bowery Mission. He was intoxicated, his face unwashed and unshaved, with clothes soiled and torn. He sank into a seat, and gazing around, seemed bewildered by the kind of place he had entered. "Rescue the Perishing" was being sung and that seemed to interest him and to recall some memories of his youth long forgotten. As the leader of the meeting told how the Lord had come to seek and to save sinners, the man listened more intently. The leader had been a soldier and had seen hard and active duty in the Civil War. He mentioned several incidents which had occurred in his experiences during the war, and gave the name of the company in which he had served. At the close of the meeting the half-intoxicated man staggered up to the leader:

Army Captain: "When were you in that company you spoke of?"

Reader 2: "Why, all through the war."

Army Captain: "Do you remember the battle of . . . ?"

Reader 2: "Perfectly!"

Army Captain: "And do you remember the name of the captain of your company at that time?"

Reader 2: "Of course. His name was . . . ."

Army Captain: "Yes, yes, you are right. I am that man. I was your captain. But look at me today, and see what a human wreck I am. Can you help your old captain? I have lost everything I had in this world through drink and now don't know where to turn."

Reader 1: The old army captain was truly converted that evening and helped by his friend to a life of usefulness and respectability. The captain often retold the story of how his former soldier was used by God to rescue his perishing soul in a mission service.

(Instruments begin playing softly)

* * * *

Reader 2: The Scriptures have much to say about Christians being "salt and light" to needy individuals in this world.

Reader 1: As we sing this familiar hymn, may we realize with greater conviction that the church's mandate is still our Lord's final command—to evangelize—to proclaim the good news of the gospel by word and deed in the power of the Holy Spirit, beginning first at our own doorsteps and then reaching out to the distant corners of the earth (Acts 1:8).

Reader 2: Give us a watchword for the hour, a thrilling word, a word of power;

A battlecry, a flaming breath that calls to conquer even death.

A word to rouse the Church from rest, to heed the Master's last request;

The call is given: Christians arise—our watchword is EVANGELIZE!   (Author unknown)

Fanny Crosby: "The Spirit of the Lord is upon me; because the Lord hath anointed me to preach good tidings unto the meek; He hath sent me to bind up the brokenhearted, to proclaim liberty to the captives, and the opening of the prison to those who are bound; to proclaim the acceptable year of the Lord, and the day of vengeance of our God; to comfort all that mourn . . . to give unto them beauty for ashes" (Isaiah 61:1-3 KJV).

* * * *

(Congregation sings "Rescue the Perishing")

See page 210, *101 Hymn Stories*

Rock of Ages

3 Characters: 2 Readers, Augustus Toplady

(Instruments begin by playing one stanza of "Rock of Ages")

Reader 1:   A British magazine invited its readers to submit a list of the 100 English hymns that stood highest in their esteem. "Rock of Ages" was the overwhelming favorite.

Reader 2:   "Rock of Ages, Cleft for Me," was written in 1776 by a young English minister named Augustus Toplady.

Reader 1:   Augustus Toplady was born at Farnham, England, in 1740. His father, an officer in the English army, was killed in action one year after his son's birth. The widowed mother eventually moved to Ireland to allow her son to be educated at the prestigious Trinity College in Dublin. It was here that sixteen year old Augustus happened to visit a gospel service held in a nearby barn. The preacher was an uneducated layman, but his simple message based on Ephesians 2:13—

Reader 2:   "Ye who sometimes were far off, are made nigh by the blood"—

Reader 1:   So gripped the heart of the young man that he determined to give his life to God and His service.

Augustus Toplady: "Strange that I who had so long sat under the means of grace in England should be brought right with God in an obscure part of Ireland, amidst a handful of people met together in a barn, and by the ministry of one who could hardly spell his own name. Surely it was the Lord's doing and is marvelous."

Reader 1:   At the age of 22 Augustus Toplady was graduated from Trinity college and was ordained as a minister of the Church of England. Though frail in body and always living under the threat of tuberculosis, he became known as a fervent evangelical preacher and writer until his death at the early age of 38. Someone described him this way—

Reader 2:   "He had an ethereal countenance. His voice was music. He had such simplicity in his words that to hear was to understand."

Reader 1: In his early ministry, Augustus Toplady was strongly attracted to the teachings of John and Charles Wesley and their Methodist followers. As time went on, however, Toplady changed his theological views and became a staunch proponent of the "election" doctrine of John Calvin as opposed to the "free will" or Arminian convictions promoted by the Wesleys. With public debates, pamphlets and sermons, Augustus Toplady and John Wesley began to carry on theological warfare:

Augustus Toplady: "I believe John Wesley to be the most rancorous hater of the gospel system that ever appeared on this island. Wesley is guilty of Satanic shamelessness—of uniting the sophistry of a Jesuit with the authority of a Pope."

Reader 1: John Wesley replied to Toplady—

Reader 2: "I dare not speak of the deep things of God in the spirit of a prizefighter or a stage player, and I do not fight with chimney sweeps . . ."

Reader 1: In 1776, just two years before his death, Toplady published his "Rock of Ages" text in *The Gospel Magazine,* of which he was the editor.

Reader 2: The poem was the climax to an article he had written attempting to prove his argument that even as England could never repay her national debt, so man through his own efforts could never satisfy the eternal justice of a Holy God. Toplady titled his poem "A Living and Dying Prayer for the Holiest Believer in the World."

Reader 1: The stanza containing the words—"Could my tears forever flow, could my zeal no languor know . . ." appears to be a satirical swipe at the Wesleyan teaching that there had to be contrite and remorseful repentance involved in one's salvation experience, to which Toplady's response was—

Reader 2: "These for sin could not atone—Thou must save and Thou alone."

Reader 1: In spite of this doctrinal controversy, Augustus Toplady was highly respected as a deeply spiritual leader. A few hours before his death he exclaimed—

Augustus Toplady: "My heart beats every day stronger and stronger for glory. Sickness is no affliction, pain no curse, death itself no dissolution. My prayers are all converted into praises."

Reader 2:   The tune, named for Pastor Toplady, was written for this text more than 50 years later by a well-known American church musician, Thomas Hastings, composer of more than 1,000 hymn tunes and texts.

(Instruments begin playing softly)

* * * *

Reader 1:   Today's hymn, despite the apparent argumentative intent of its author, has been preserved by God for more than two centuries to minister spiritual blessing to believers of both Calvinistic and Arminian theological persuasions. It reinforces these foundational truths of Scripture:

Reader 2:   "Salvation is found in no one else, for there is no other name under heaven given to men by which we must be saved" (Acts 4:12).

Reader 1:   "But let all who take refuge in You be glad; let them ever sing for joy. Spread Your protection over them, that those who love Your name may rejoice in You" (Psalm 5:11).

Reader 2:   As we sing this favorite hymn, may these words by Augustus Toplady also be our earnest plea—

Augustus Toplady: "When I soar to worlds unknown, and behold Thee on Thy throne—
Rock of Ages, cleft for me, let me hide myself in Thee."

* * * *

(Congregation sings "Rock of Ages")

See page 215, *101 Hymn Stories*

Drama 41

Silent Night! Holy Night!

2 Characters: 2 Readers

*(Instruments begin by playing softly one stanza of
"Silent Night! Holy Night!")*

Reader 1: Undoubtedly the favorite of all Christmas carols, "Silent Night! Holy Night!" is loved by both young and old for its serene and beautiful portrayal of the Savior's humble birth.

Reader 2: Yet when the hymn was written for their own village parishioners by two humble church leaders, Father Joseph Mohr (MOR) and organist Franz Grüber (GROO-ber), little did they realize how universal its influence would eventually be.

Reader 1: It was while serving as an assistant priest in 1818 at the newly erected Church of St. Nicholas in Oberndorf in the region of Tyrol (TI-rol), Austria, high in the beautiful Alps, that Father Mohr wrote the text for "Silent Night! Holy Night!"

Reader 2: Father Mohr had often talked to Franz Grüber, the village schoolmaster and church organist, about the fact that the ideal Christmas hymn has never yet been written.

Reader 1: With this thought in mind, and after he had received the disheartening news that his church organ would not function, Father Mohr decided that he must write his own Christmas hymn immediately in order to have music for the special Christmas Eve Mass to avoid disappointing his faithful flock. Upon completing the text, he took his words to Franz Grüber, who exclaimed when he saw them—

Reader 2: "Friend Mohr, you have found it—the right song— God be praised!"

Reader 1: Soon Grüber completed his task of composing an appropriate melody for the new text. His simple but beautiful music blended perfectly with the spirit of

Father Mohr's words. The carol was completed in time for the Christmas Eve Mass, and Father Mohr and Franz Grüber sang their new hymn to the accompaniment of Grüber's guitar.

Reader 2:   The carol made a deep impact upon the mountain parishioners just as it has on succeeding generations. The passing of time seems only to add to its appeal.

Reader 1:   A few days later, when the organ repair man came to the little village church, he was impressed by a copy of the Christmas carol and decided to promote it all around the region of Tyrol. Before long "Silent Night! Holy Night!" was sung throughout Austria and Germany and became known as a Tyrolean folk song.

Reader 2:   It was first heard in the United States in 1839 when a family of Tyrolean singers, the Rainers, used the music during their concert tour. Soon it was translated into English as well as all the major languages of the world, and it has become a universal favorite wherever songs of the Christmas message are enjoyed.

(Instruments begin playing softly)

* * * *

Reader 1:   As we sing this much-loved carol together, allow its peaceful strains to help us worship in awe as did the shepherds.

Reader 2:   And may we sing our alleluias with the "heavenly hosts" for the "redeeming grace" made possible by our Savior's birth on that silent, holy night 2,000 years ago.

* * * *

(Congregation sings "Silent Night! Holy Night!"—perhaps with guitar accompaniment)

See page 221, *101 Hymn Stories*

Drama 42

Stand Up for Jesus

3 Characters: 2 Readers, Rev. Dudley Tyng

*(Instruments begin by playing a portion of
"Stand Up for Jesus"—Webb Tune)*

Reader 1: It was in 1858 that a great city-wide revival swept
through Philadelphia. It was called "The work of God
in Philadelphia." Of the participating ministers, none
was more powerful than the 29-year-old Episcopalian,
Dudley Tyng (Ting).

Reader 2: Tyng was known as a bold, fearless and uncom-
promising preacher with great influence on the other
spiritual leaders around him. His father, the Rev. Ste-
phen Tyng, was for many years pastor of the large Episcopalian Church of the Epiphany (E-PIF-a-ny) in
Philadelphia. After serving a time as his father's assistant, young Dudley succeeded his father as the senior
minister.

Reader 1: However, some of the more fashionable members
soon became upset with their young pastor because of
his strong, straightforward preaching. He resigned this
pulpit and organized the Church of the Covenant with
a group of his faithful followers.

Reader 2: In addition to his duties in this new and growing
congregation, Dudley began holding noonday services
at the downtown YMCA. Great crowds came to hear
this dynamic young preacher.

Reader 1: At noon, March 30, 1858, over 5,000 men gathered
for a mass men's meeting to hear young Tyng preach
from Exodus 10:11—

Dudley Tyng: "Ye that are men, go and serve the Lord."

Reader 1: Over 1,000 of these men committed their lives to
Christ. The sermon was described as "one of the most
successful of the times." As a climax, the young preacher shouted out . . .

Dudley Tyng: "I must tell my Master's errand, and I would rather that this right arm were amputated at the trunk than that I should come short of my duty to you in delivering God's message."

Reader 2:   The very next week, while visiting in the country and watching the operation of a corn threshing machine in a barn, young Tyng accidentally caught his loose sleeve between the cogs; the arm was lacerated severely with the main artery severed and the median nerve injured.

Reader 1:   Four days later severe infection developed. As a result of shock and a great loss of blood, the Rev. Dudley Tyng died on April 19, 1858.

Reader 2:   On his death bed when asked by a group of sorrowing friends and fellow ministers for a final statement, he whispered feebly . . .

Dudley Tyng: "Let us all stand up for Jesus."

Reader 1:   The next Sunday Tyng's close friend, the Rev. George Duffield, pastor of the Temple Presbyterian Church in Philadelphia, delivered a tribute to his departed colleague. He chose as his text Ephesians 6:14—

Reader 2:   "Stand, therefore, having your loins girded about with truth, and having on the breastplate of righteousness."

Reader 1:   Pastor Duffield closed his sermon by reading a poem that he had just finished writing. He told his people that he had been inspired by the dying words of his esteemed friend. Rev. Duffield's Sunday school superintendent was so impressed by these verses that he had them printed for distribution throughout the entire congregation. The editor of a Baptist magazine received one of these pamphlets and promptly gave the text wider circulation.

Reader 2:   And from that time to the present, the hymn "Stand Up for Jesus" has found its way into the hearts and hymnals of God's people around the world.

(Congregation sings "Stand Up for Jesus")

See page 236, *101 Hymn Stories*

Sweet Hour of Prayer

4 Characters: 2 Readers, William Walford, Pastor Thomas Salmon

Reader 1:   Devout believers in Christ have always recognized the absolute necessity of maintaining intimate relations with God through His ordained channel of prayer. It has often been said that . . .

Reader 2:   "Prayer is as basic to spiritual life as breathing is to our natural lives."

Reader 1:   Or as others have stated . . .

Reader 2:   "Prayer is not merely an occasional impulse to which we respond when in trouble; for the Christian, prayer is a normal habit of living—a necessary source of strength and guidance for each day."

(Instruments play a portion of "Sweet Hour of Prayer")

Reader 1:   For more than a century, "Sweet Hour of Prayer" has been one of our best-known hymns for reminding us of the importance of daily communion with God.

Reader 2:   For some time it was reported that the text was written by a William Walford, a blind lay preacher and owner of a small trinket shop in the quaint little village of Coleshill, England.

Reader 1:   One day Thomas Salmon, the pastor of the Congregational church in the village, is said to have stopped at Walford's shop for a visit with his blind friend. He was likely greeted by Walford in this manner—

William Walford: "Oh, Pastor Salmon, how good of you to visit me. God has just given me some new words on the subject of prayer. Would you like to hear them? Perhaps you would be willing to write them down while I say them for you—"

Reader 2:   Pastor Salmon listened intently as his blind friend began reciting all three stanzas of his new prayer poem.

William Walford: 1.   Sweet hour of prayer, sweet hour of prayer, that calls me from a world of care,

And bids me at my Father's throne make all my wants
and wishes known!
In seasons of distress and grief my soul has often found
relief,
And oft escaped the tempter's snare by thy return,
sweet hour of prayer.

2. Sweet hour of prayer, sweet hour of prayer, thy
wings shall my petition bear
To Him whose truth and faithfulness engage the
waiting soul to bless;
And since He bids me seek His face, believe His Word
and trust His grace,
I'll cast on Him my ev'ry care, and wait for thee, sweet
hour of prayer.

3. Sweet hour of prayer, sweet hour of prayer, may I
thy consolation share,
Till from Mount Pisgah's (PIS-gah's) lofty height I view
my home and take my flight.
This robe of flesh I'll drop, and rise to seize the
everlasting prize,
And shout, while passing through the air, "Farewell,
farewell, sweet hour of prayer."

Pastor Thomas Salmon: "Oh, brother Walford, those are unusually fine words. The first two stanzas remind us so
well of the blessings of prayer—that there is relief for our
troubled lives and the assurance of a God who is concerned with our every need. And that final verse antici-
pates so well the day when we will no longer need to
pray, for we'll be at home in heaven where our prayers
will all be turned to praise. I also like your interesting
reference to Mount Pisgah—the place where God instructed Moses to go and simply view the promised land (Deu-
teronomy 34:1-4). We too can enjoy the prospects of
heaven even now as we spend time in communion with
our Lord."

Reader 1: Several years later, the Reverend Thomas
Salmon visited the United States and showed this

poem to the editor of the *New York Observer Magazine*. The poem first appeared in the September 13, 1845 issue.

Reader 2:   It was here that Pastor Salmon described the poem as "the product of William Walford, a blind fellow-clergyman from the little village of Coleshill, England."

Reader 1:   In recent years, however, there have been questions raised about the real author of this text. Students of hymnody have done considerable research and have been unable to establish with certainty that a blind lay preacher named William Walford ever lived in Coleshill at the same time when this text was written.

Reader 2:   The possibility is suggested that Pastor Thomas Salmon, in his enthusiasm for getting the poem published, exaggerated and popularized some of his data when promoting the poem to the editor of the New York publication.

Reader 1:   Regardless of the actual author or origin of this text, we must conclude that "Sweet Hour of Prayer" has been widely used of God for many years to challenge believers with the truth that time spent each day in communion with the Lord is a spiritually enriching hour in our lives.

Reader 2:   "There is no sweeter time than this, the hour we spend with Jesus;

To taste with Him eternal bliss, the hour we spend with Jesus."   (Author unknown)

Reader 1:   The tune was composed especially for this text nearly 20 years later by William Bradbury, the noted American composer of early gospel music. Lifted on the wings of Bradbury's melody, this simple but heart-felt hymn was soon sung by Christians around the world with much spiritual blessing.

(Instruments begin playing softly)

* * * *

Reader 2:   May the singing of this hymn prompt us to cry out with the disciples of old—"Lord, teach us to pray" (Luke

11:1). Then may it be our daily resolve to say with this hymn writer—

Together: "AND SINCE HE BIDS ME SEEK HIS FACE, I'LL CAST ON HIM MY EVERY CARE—SWEET HOUR OF PRAYER."

✱ ✱ ✱ ✱

(Congregation sings "Sweet Hour of Prayer")

See page 258, *101 More Hymn Stories*

- "I can take my telescope and look millions of miles into space, but I can lay it aside and go into my room, shut the door, get down on my knees in earnest prayer, and see more of heaven and get closer to God than I can assisted by all the telescopes and material agencies on earth."   —Sir Isaac Newton

- "No one is poor who can by prayer open the storehouse of God."   —Louis Paul Lehman

- "God is on His throne, I am at His footstool and there is only a knee's distance between them."
  —John Knox

Drama 44

Take My Life and Let It Be

3 Characters: 2 Readers, Frances Ridley Havergal

Frances Ridley Havergal: "Take my silver and my gold, not a mite would I withhold . . ."

Reader 1:   These words of commitment were part of a series of couplets written by one of England's finest hymn writers of the past century, Frances Ridley Havergal, who was known as the "Consecration Poet." They form a hymn which still speaks pointedly to us today—

(Instruments play a verse of "Take My Life and Let It Be")

Reader 2:   "Take My Life and Let It Be Consecrated Lord to Thee" has been widely used for more than a century to challenge believers with a total surrender to Christ and the embracing of His Lordship in their lives.

Reader 1:   Frances Ridley Havergal was born in 1836 at Astley, England. At the age of four she began reading and memorizing the Bible. By the time she was seven she was already writing her thoughts in verse and soon had committed to memory much of the New Testament and the book of Psalms.

Reader 2:   The testimony of her many friends was always that the beauty of a consecrated life was never more perfectly revealed than in Frances Havergal's daily living. Wherever Frances saw spiritual and physical needs, she responded with genuine concern.

Reader 1:   Throughout her brief lifetime of 43 years, Miss Havergal was frail and in poor health; yet she lived an active life and was an avid student, writer and composer. She was conversant in at least six modern languages as well as Hebrew and Greek.

Reader 2:   In her childhood years Frances lived in morbid fear that she would not be counted among God's elect. However, during early adolescence she had a vital conversion experience and later wrote—

Frances Ridley Havergal: "Then I committed my soul to the

Savior—and earth and heaven seemed brighter from that moment."

Reader 1: Miss Havergal was an accomplished musician with a voice so pleasing that she was much sought after as a concert soloist. She was also known as an excellent classical pianist. Although these musical talents as well as an engaging, vibrant personality would have assured her of much worldly acclaim, "singing and serving Jesus" were always her life's mission.

Frances Ridley Havergal: "One day I went for a little visit of five days. There were ten persons in the house; some unconverted and long prayed for, others converted but not rejoicing Christians. After the first day I prayed, 'Lord, give me all in this house.' And He just did! Before I left, everyone had got a blessing. The last night of my visit I was too happy to sleep and passed most of the night in renewal of my own consecration . . . and suddenly these little couplets chimed in my heart one after another and I wrote them down—

Take my life and let it be consecrated, Lord, to Thee!
Take my moments and my days . . . let them flow in
     ceaseless praise.
Take my hands and let them move at the impulse of
     Thy love.
Take my feet and let them be swift and beautiful for
     Thee.
Take my voice and let me sing always, only, for my
     King.
Take my lips and let them be filled with messages for
     Thee.
Take my silver and my gold . . . not a mite would I
     withhold.
Take my love . . . my God, I pour at Thy feet its treasure
     store.
Take myself and I will be ever, only, all for Thee."

Reader 2: Several years later while straightening her desk, Frances came upon the lines she had written that night.

Frances Ridley Havergal: "I had forgotten them . . . but as I read through each one again, this line leaped out at me—*Take my silver and my gold, not a mite would I with-hold.* Then the Lord directed me to another little step of faith. I had always been very fond of the many pieces of fine jewelry and other ornaments that I had . . . some of them family heirlooms. But that day I gathered all I could together . . .brooches, rings, necklaces, even a little jewel box that was fit for a countess, and shipped them off to the church Missionary House to be sold for evangelizing the lost in heathen lands. Nearly 50 articles were sent . . . and I don't think I ever packed a box with more pleasure! After that my little couplets, which had spoken so clearly to my own soul, have become a hymn that has since moved others as well to a deeper consecration of their lives to God."

Reader 1:   Other favorite hymns by Francis Havergal that are still widely sung include:

Reader 2:   "I Gave My Life for Thee"; "Like a River Glorious"; "I Am Trusting Thee, Lord Jesus"; "Who Is On the Lord's Side?"; "True-Hearted, Whole-Hearted"; and "Lord, Speak to Me"—all of which reflect the joy of genuine commitment to God and His service.

(Instruments begin playing softly)

✳   ✳   ✳   ✳

Reader 1:   In 1879, at the age of 43, Frances Ridley Havergal left this life triumphantly with these words upon her lips—

Reader 2:   "Jesus, I will trust Thee, trust Thee with my soul;
Guilty, lost, and helpless—Thou hast made me whole."

Reader 1:   In this day of indulgent, self-centered living, how important it is that we as God's people allow the truth of these words by Frances Havergal to challenge anew our commitment to the God we worship and serve—

Reader 2:   "Take myself and I will be ever, only, all for Thee."

✳   ✳   ✳   ✳

(Congregation sings "Take My Life and Let It Be")

See page 239, *101 Hymn Stories*

The Church's One Foundation

4 Characters: 3 Readers, Rev. Samuel Stone

Reader 1: "I AM THE CHURCH!

Reader 2: The great Creator drew the plans for me within His heart of love; my one and only foundation is His Son— whose body was nailed to a tree. From my belfry rings out the call for worship to countless multitudes of all ages; my door swings open to all of every race and every age—bidding them welcome.

Reader 3: In my sanctuary there is peace for tired minds, rest for weary bodies, compassion for suffering humanity, forgiveness for repentant sinners, communion for saints, Christ for all who seek Him.

Reader 1: I AM THE CHURCH!

Reader 2: Without me, civilization must crumble.

Reader 3: With me is eternity!"   (Author unknown)

Reader 1: The church is truly God's ordained agency for proclaiming His redemptive message and for advancing His Kingdom here on earth. Yet the church of Jesus Christ has been the object of harassment and persecution since its inception on the day of Pentecost to the present.

Reader 2: Our featured hymn for this service was written during the past century by an Anglican minister who became deeply concerned about the liberal attacks that were being made against the great cardinal doctrines of the church.

Rev. Samuel Stone: "I desired to write a hymn text that would reaffirm for the worshipers of my day the most basic truth about the church—that its very foundation is its founder—Jesus Christ."

Reader 1: And still today we sing the truth of this hymn with great conviction whenever its stirring music is heard in a worship service—

(Instruments play a portion of "The Church's One Foundation")

Reader 1: This familiar and stately hymn, "The Church's One Foundation," was written by a Church of England pastor, Samuel Stone.

Reader 2: In 1866 there was much turmoil within the Anglican state church because of an influential English bishop's writings questioning the accuracy of parts of the Old Testament.

Reader 1: The book, *The Pentateuch and the Book of Joshua, Critically Examined,* soon produced theological warfare as the controversy became widespread throughout the entire state church.

Reader 2: Pastor Stone became deeply stirred by this conflict within the churches. To combat these attacks of skeptical modern scholarship, which he felt would soon divide and destroy the church, he wrote a collection of 12 hymns reaffirming the Apostle's Creed. Today's hymn was based on this statement from the creed—

Reader 3: "I believe in the Holy Catholic or Universal Church . . . and Christ is the head of His body, the Church,"

Rev. Samuel Stone: "It is my strong conviction that the unity of the Church must rest solely on a recognition of the Lordship of Christ as its head and master, and not on the changing views and interpretations of men."

Reader 1: The hymn text soon became widely popular throughout Great Britain. It was also translated into a number of other languages and was sung around the world.

Reader 2: Two years after Samuel Stone wrote this text, all of the Church of England bishops assembled in London for an impressive theological gathering known as the Lambeth Conference. Stone's hymn was chosen as the processional and theme song for that historic meeting. The hymn's influence is said to have had a unifying effect upon these leaders by directing their attention to Christ and away from their skepticism and doctrinal differences.

Reader 1: The composer of this stirring music was Samuel Wesley, grandson of the renowned eighteenth century hymn writer, Charles Wesley. Samuel was the composer of much quality church music and many hymn tunes still widely used today.

Reader 2: His music for this hymn was first matched with Pastor Stone's text for use at the Bishop's Lambeth Conference.

(Instruments begin playing softly)

* * * *

Reader 1: As we sing this moving hymn, may we be convinced anew of this basic truth—

Reader 2: The only sure foundation for our lives, our homes, and our churches . . .

Reader 3: IS JESUS CHRIST, OUR LORD!

* * * *

(Congregation sings "The Church's One Foundation")

See page 242, *101 Hymn Stories*

- "The church is not a gallery for the exhibition of eminent Christians, but a school for the education of imperfect ones."   —Henry Ward Beecher

- "A church should be a powerhouse, where sluggish spirits can get recharged and reanimated."
                                        —Samuel A. Eliot

Drama 46

The Love of God

3 Characters: 2 Readers, Pastor Frederick Lehman

Reader 1: "As the Father has loved Me, so have I loved you. Now remain in my love."

Reader 2: What an amazing statement is this in John 15:9. Here our Lord compared the very quality of love that the Father had for Him to the love He had for His disciples—and also for you and me.

Reader 1: And the command that He gives to His followers of every generation is to live continually in the power and enjoyment of that divine love.

Reader 2: * "O love of God, how rich and pure! How measureless and strong! It shall forevermore endure—the saints' and angels' song."

(Instruments play the chorus of "The Love of God")

Reader 1: This well-known hymn, "The Love of God," was written in the year 1917 by a Nazarene pastor named Frederick Lehman.

Reader 2: Pastor Lehman served Nazarene Churches in Indiana and Illinois before moving to Kansas City, where he became involved in starting the Nazarene Publishing House. Throughout his ministry, Mr. Lehman wrote numerous poems and songs, which were published in five volumes titled *Songs That Are Different*. "The Love of God" first appeared in Volume Two of that series, two years after its writing.

Reader 1: Frederick Lehman's faithful and fruitful ministry for God ended at his home in Pasadena, California in the year 1953 at the age of 85. But the Christian church will always be indebted to Pastor Lehman for these first two stanzas and for the music of this beloved hymn—

(Instruments play softly behind the reading)

---

* * * *

Reader 2:

1. "The love of God is greater far than tongue or pen
   can ever tell,

   It goes beyond the highest star and reaches to the
   lowest hell;

   The guilty pair, bowed down with care, God gave His
   Son to win:

   His erring child He reconciled and pardoned from his sin.

2. When years of time shall pass away and earthly
   thrones and kingdoms fall,

   When men, who here refuse to pray, on rocks and hills
   and mountains call.

   God's love so sure shall still endure, all measureless
   and strong:

   Redeeming grace to Adam's race—The saints' and
   angels' song."

* * * *

Reader 1:   The third stanza of this hymn, however, has quite a
different history. It is believed that the unusually descriptive words for this verse were adapted from a poem
that had been written in the eleventh century.

Reader 2:   This Jewish poem, known as the "Hadamut," (HA-
da-MUT) was composed in the year 1096 by a Jewish
German leader named Rabbi Mayer. Throughout this
lengthy poem of 90 verses, the theme of God's eternal
love and concern for His chosen but persecuted people
is dominant.

Reader 1:   From one section of this poem the present third
stanza of the hymn was apparently adapted. The original version reads as follows:

Reader 2:   "Were the sky of parchment made, a quill each
reed, each twig and blade,

Could we with ink the ocean fill, were every man a
scribe of skill;

The marvelous story of God's great glory would still
remain untold;

For He, most high the earth and sky created alone of old."

Reader 1:   The revised lines of this Jewish poem were one day found in a mental institution penciled on the wall of the room of a patient who had died. The general opinion has been that during times of sanity this unknown patient adapted from the Jewish poem the now familiar third stanza of "The Love of God" hymn.

Reader 2:   * 3. "Could we with ink the ocean fill and were the skies of parchment made,

Were ev'ry stalk on earth a quill and ev'ry man a scribe by trade,

To write the love of God above would drain the ocean dry,

Nor could the scroll contain the whole though stretched from sky to sky."

Reader 1:   In 1948 Pastor Frederick Lehman wrote a pamphlet titled *History of the Song "The Love of God."* In it he recalls these circumstances—

Pastor Frederick Lehman: "While at a camp meeting in a mid-western state some 50 years ago in our early ministry, an evangelist climaxed his message by quoting the last stanza of this song. The profound depths of the lines moved me to preserve the words for future generations."

Reader 1:   Later Mr. Lehman moved to California and for a time while not pastoring a church, he was forced to take a job doing manual labor.

Pastor Frederick Lehman: "Not until we had come to California did the urge to complete and preserve these words find fulfillment, and that at a time when various situations forced me to do hard manual labor. One day during short intervals of inattention to my work, I picked up a scrap of paper and, seated upon an empty lemon box pushed against the wall, with just a stub of pencil completed the first two stanzas and chorus of the song. The third stanza, written nearly 1,000 years earlier by a Jewish songwriter, was then added to my first two stanzas. This was in the year 1917. Later my daughter Claudia completed the harmonization of my tune for these words."

(Instruments begin playing softly)

✱ ✱ ✱ ✱

Reader 1:   And from that time to the present, "'The Love of God" has provided Christian people with a choice vehicle for expressing gratitude to their Heavenly Father for His divine love, affirming the teaching of Scripture—

Reader 2:   That we have been loved with an everlasting love and drawn to God with His lovingkindness—an unfailing love that continues to surround all those who trust in Him (Jeremiah 31:3; Psalm 32:10).

Reader 1:   As we mature in the Christian faith, may this prayer by the apostle Paul for the first century believers become increasingly true in our lives today—

Reader 2:   "That you, being rooted and established in love, may have the power, with all the saints, to grasp how wide and long and high and deep is the love of Christ"— and "that your love may abound still more and more in knowledge and all discernment" (Ephesians 3:17, 18; Philippians 1:9).

✱ ✱ ✱ ✱

(Congregation sings "The Love of God")

See page 271, *101 More Hymn Stories*

The Ninety and Nine

3 Characters: 2 Readers, Ira Sankey

Reader 1: The ministries of Dwight L. Moody and Ira Sankey in city-wide evangelistic campaigns had a great spiritual impact in this country and throughout Great Britain during the last quarter of the nineteenth century.

Reader 2: From these meetings emerged a new type of sacred music known as the "gospel song." As Ira Sankey often stated—

Ira Sankey: "This is music that is calculated to awaken the careless, to melt the hardened, and to guide inquiring souls to Jesus Christ."

Reader 1: It was during a time of Moody and Sankey's extensive ministering throughout the British Isles that Ira Sankey composed the music for one of his best known gospel songs, "The Ninety and Nine!"

(Instruments play "The Ninety and Nine" softly while the story of the hymn's origin is told)

✳ ✳ ✳ ✳

Ira Sankey: "Mr. Moody and I were riding in a train one morning from Glasgow to Edinburgh, Scotland, to conduct a service in the Free Assembly Hall of Edinburgh. I stopped to purchase a newspaper in the train depot, hoping to get some news from America. While reading the paper during the ride, I discovered a most interesting poem written for children by a Scottish woman named Elizabeth Clephane. I recalled that this was the same lady who had written the words for the fine hymn "Beneath the Cross of Jesus." I tried to show the poem to Mr. Moody but he was too busy preparing his sermon. Finally, I simply tore out the poem and placed it in my vest pocket and thought no more of it."

Reader 2: At the meeting that afternoon in Edinburgh, the theme of Mr. Moody's message was "The Good Shepherd," based on the account in Luke 15. Concluding his sermon, the evangelist suddenly announced—"Mr. Sankey will now sing an appropriate closing number."

Ira Sankey: "Startled, I could recall nothing that seemed appropriate for that message. Then I remembered the little poem that I had put in my vest pocket. I placed the newspaper clipping on the folding organ before me, breathed a quick prayer for divine help, struck the chord of A flat, and began to sing the words while note by note the tune was given to me; and that same tune with Elizabeth Clephane's words has remained unchanged to the present time. As I neared the end of the song, Mr. Moody was in tears and so was I. When he arose to give the invitation for salvation, many lost sheep responded to the call of Christ. It was one of the most intense and inspiring moments of my entire life."

* * * *

Reader 1: Some time later Moody and Sankey conducted a service in the quaint town of Melrose, Scotland, the home of the author of this poem, Elizabeth Clephane, who had died three years earlier. But Elizabeth's two sisters were in the audience when the noted Ira Sankey sang the "Ninety and Nine" once more.

Reader 2: One can imagine their delight and surprise when they heard their departed sister's words set to Sankey's music and learned of the spiritual impact that this hymn had already had in the spread of the gospel—even as it has had to the present time.

Reader 1: For nearly 30 years Moody and Sankey were inseparable in their evangelistic crusades. They were often called the David and Jonathan of the gospel ministry. Moody—the uneducated, impulsive but magnetic personality—and Sankey—the refined, cultured musician who could inspire large audiences while leading and singing from a humble pump organ.

Reader 2: Ira Sankey never forgot his first meeting with Mr. Moody—

Ira Sankey: "I had been sent as a delegate to the 1870 YMCA convention at Indianapolis, Indiana. After the first few

services, which had been rather dull, someone suggested that I lead the singing, which I did. The response
was most enthusiastic. At the close of the convention, I
was told that a Mr. Moody wanted to meet me. As I
drew near Mr. Moody, he stepped forward, took me by
the hand, and looked at me with that keen, piercing
fashion of his, as if reading my very soul. I can still
recall his first abrupt greeting—"

Reader 2: "Where are you from?"

Ira Sankey: "Pennsylvania."

Reader 2: "Are you married?"

Ira Sankey: "I am."

Reader 2: "How many children do you have?"

Ira Sankey: "Two."

Reader 2: "What is your business?"

Ira Sankey: "I am a government officer in the Internal Reve-
nue Office."

Reader 2: "Well, you"ll have to give it up. I have been looking for you for the last eight years. You will have to
come to Chicago and help me with my work."

Reader 1: After several months of prayerful indecision, Ira
Sankey resigned his government position and moved
to Chicago. There he began a ministry with this remarkable evangelist that lasted nearly 30 years.

Reader 2: It was here that Ira Sankey earned the title as the
Father of the Gospel Song with his writing and publishing of much gospel music.

Reader 1: Gospel songs began in America shortly after the
close of the Civil War. They were an outgrowth of the
camp meetings that became especially popular throughout the South during this time.

Reader 2: In addition to the preaching, the most important
aspect of these meetings was the singing. The words of
these songs were simply stated truths while the tunes,
often borrowed from the popular secular songs of the
day, were easily learned and sung by rote.

Reader 1: From these meetings there developed a large reper-
tory of simple folk hymns and spiritual songs. Some of
these early songs are still sung and enjoyed today.

(Instruments begin playing softly)

* * * *

Reader 2:   But no gospel song has been used more extensively in evangelistic meetings than "The Ninety and Nine," hurriedly composed by Ira Sankey with the Spirit's leading at a time when it was urgently needed. And still today it speaks to us of that Good Shepherd who is earnestly seeking the one who has strayed from the Father's tender love.

* * * *

(Congregation or soloist sings "The Ninety and Nine")

See page 250, *101 Hymn Stories*

- "All my theology is reduced to this narrow compass—Christ Jesus came into this world to save sinners."   —Archibald Alexander

- "Salvation is by atonement, not attainment; by believing, not achieving."   —Author unknown

Drama 48

The Old Rugged Cross

3 Characters: 2 Readers, Rev. George Bennard

Reader 1: "Let us fix our eyes on Jesus, the author and perfecter of our faith, who for the joy set before Him endured the cross, scorning its shame, and sat down at the right hand of the throne of God" (Hebrews 12:2).

Reader 2: The hymn we are considering in this service is generally regarded as one of the most popular of all twentieth century gospel hymns. Its popularity peaked during the Billy Sunday-Homer Rodeheaver evangelistic campaigns and the early decades of the twentieth century. Yet this hymn is still a sentimental favorite of both old and young alike.

(Instruments play a portion of "The Old Rugged Cross")

Reader 2: "The Old Rugged Cross," was written in the year 1913 by a Methodist evangelist, George Bennard (Ben-NARD).

Reader 1: George Bennard was born in Ohio but later settled in Iowa. At a young age he made his personal acceptance of Christ as Savior. Following his father's death, George found it necessary at just sixteen years of age to assume the sole support of his mother and four sisters. This made it impossible for him to pursue further education for the Christian ministry.

Reader 2: Instead he entered and became active in the ranks of the Salvation Army. Bennard and his first wife served for a number of years as officers in this organization. The composer often stated that he gave much of the credit for the inspiration which led to the writing of "The Old Rugged Cross" to his experiences in this ministry.

Reader 1: Although self-taught, Bennard was eventually ordained by the Methodist Episcopal Church, where his devoted ministry was highly esteemed for many years. He became involved in conducting revival services, especially throughout the states of Michigan and New York.

Reader 2: During this time he passed through a particularly trying experience which caused him to reflect seriously about the significance of the cross and what the apostle Paul meant when he spoke of "entering into the fellowship of Christ's suffering" (Philippians 3:10). George Bennard began to spend long hours in study, prayer and meditation until one day he could say—

Rev. George Bennard: "I saw the Christ of the cross as if I were seeing John 3:16 leave the printed page, take form and act out the meaning of redemption. The more I contemplated these truths the more convinced I became that the cross was far more than just a religious symbol but rather the very heart of the gospel."

Reader 1: During these days of spiritual struggle the theme for "The Old Rugged Cross" began to shape itself in his mind. But an inner voice seemed to keep telling him to wait. Then the press of duties in preparing for additional campaigns throughout New York prevented Bennard from finishing the hymn at that time. Finally, however, he began to concentrate anew on his project, and soon the words and melody began to flow more freely from his heart.

Rev. George Bennard: "The inspiration came to me one day in 1913, when I was staying in Albion, Michigan. I composed the melody first. The words that I originally wrote were imperfect. The words of the finished hymn were put into my heart in answer to my own personal need. Shortly thereafter it was introduced at special meetings in Pokagon (Po-KA-gon), Michigan, on June 7th 1913."

Reader 2: From the penciled copy of Bennard's manuscript, the hymn was first sung by a choir of just five voices at the little Pokagon Church. An "Old Rugged Cross Day" is still observed annually at this church, and on a large stone nearby are carved the names of the five original singers of the hymn and the significance of that memorable Sunday in 1913.

Reader 1: Shortly after writing the hymn George Bennard

sent a manuscript copy to Charles Gabriel, one of the leading gospel hymn writers of this period. Gabriel's prophetic words . . .

Reader 2: "You will certainly hear from this song, Mr. Bennard—"

Reader 1: Were soon realized as "The Old Rugged Cross" became in this country one of the most widely published songs, either sacred or secular. It has been recorded more than any other hymn. In the jails and prisons throughout America it has become known as "the prisoner's anthem."

Reader 2: Following the writing of his hymn, George Bennard continued his evangelistic ministries for 40 additional years. He wrote a number of other gospel hymns, but none ever received the response of "The Old Rugged Cross." In 1958, at the age of 85, George Bennard exchanged his "cross for a crown."

Reader 1: Bennard spent the last years of his life at his home near Reed City, Michigan, which he called "the side of the road." Near this home there still stands a twelve foot high cross with the words—"THE OLD RUGGED CROSS—HOME OF GEORGE BENNARD, COMPOSER OF THIS BELOVED HYMN."

(Instruments begin playing softly)

*   *   *   *

Reader 2: Only eternity will reveal fully the number of lives that have been influenced for God by this one simply worded and easily sung gospel hymn. Although we do not worship the cross as such but rather the Christ of the cross, we cannot ponder the great truths of Christ's atonement without a keen awareness of the centrality of the cross in God's plan of redemption for lost mankind.

*   *   *   *

(Congregation sings "The Old Rugged Cross")

See page 254, *101 Hymn Stories*

There Is a Green Hill Far Away

3 Characters: 2 Readers, Mrs. Alexander

Reader 1: It has been stated that we grasp a great deal of what we learn through the songs we hear and sing.

Reader 2: We have often heard it quoted: "Give me the making of the songs of a nation, and I care not who makes its laws" (Andrew Fletcher, 1665-1716).

Reader 1: And in times of deep spiritual need our practical theology is often a simple expression of our hymnology—"'Tis so sweet to trust in Jesus . . ."

Reader 2: A mark of greatness is the ability to make profound truths visually understandable to a child. Such was the gift of Mrs. Cecil Frances Alexander, generally regarded as one of the finest of all women hymn writers.

(Instruments play a portion of "There Is a Green Hill Far Away")

Reader 2: Mrs. Alexander's hymn, "There Is a Green hill Far Away," though intended for children, has also been widely used by adult congregations for more than a century. Like so many of our enduring hymns, its simplicity still speaks to adults.

Reader 1: Mrs. Alexander was born in Ireland in 1818. Before her marriage to Dr. William Alexander, a distinguished Anglican churchman who later became archbishop for all of Ireland, Frances was actively involved in the Sunday school movement that was just beginning to spread throughout Great Britain at this time. Mrs. Alexander never lost her love for children and the desire to teach them sound spiritual truths, which she maintained could best be done through the use of worthy hymns.

Reader 2: Two years before her marriage, Frances published a volume of children's hymns that probably has never been excelled by a similar collection. It covered a wide range of doctrinal subjects such as the Ten

Commandments, the Apostles' Creed, the Lord's Prayer, and many other biblical themes.

Reader 1: Since most of the 400 poems and hymns written by Mrs. Alexander throughout her life were intended for children, the language is always direct and easily understood. "There Is a Green Hill Far Away," though doctrinal in content, is so simply stated that even small children can visualize and comprehend the very moving message of Christ's atonement.

Reader 2: The hymn was written for Mrs. Alexander's own Sunday school class to teach them the meaning of the phrase from the Apostles' Creed—"Suffered under Pontius Pilate, was crucified, dead and buried."

Mrs. Alexander: "It was my intent to take this great truth regarding Christ's sacrificial atonement and make it have personal and practical meaning to our boys and girls. I especially wanted to personalize for each youngster such foundational truths of the gospel as 'He died that we might be forgiven, He died to make us good, that we might go at last to heav'n—saved by His precious blood.'"

Reader 1: How important it is for each of us to allow the Holy Spirit to apply the precepts of God's Word to our daily living rather than giving a mere vague assent to such truths. And it is also vitally important that the songs we sing and hear teach the attributes of God with accuracy, clarity and scriptural integrity.

Reader 2: God's greatness, for example, far exceeds the thought of merely being "somebody bigger than you and I."

Reader 1: Prayer and communion with the Almighty are far more necessary than just "having a little talk with Jesus."

Reader 2: Or the anticipation of eternal glory for a child of God should do much more to thrill his soul than simply present the prospect of "I'll fly away."

Reader 1: After her marriage at the age of 32, Mrs. Alexander continued her writing and concerns for the Christian ministries. She became actively involved with her husband's parish duties. Her life was so characterized with deeds of helpfulness and charity that her husband once wrote this tribute—

Reader 2:   "From one poor home to another she went. Christ was ever with her, and all felt her godly influence."

Reader 1:   And those who knew Mrs. Alexander intimately often claimed that her daily life style was even more beautiful than her lovely hymns and poetry. She was a very humble person who disdained praise for her many accomplishments.

Reader 2:   On one occasion, however, when someone wrote to tell of the change in heart and life that had come to a wayward person through one of her hymns, she sprang to her feet, joyfully exclaiming . . .

Mrs. Alexander: "Thank God, I do like to hear that!"

Reader 1:   The composer of the music for "There Is a Green Hill Far Away" was George Stebbins, a well-known name in the field of early American gospel music.

Reader 2:   Mr. Stebbins composed the tune 30 years after Mrs. Alexander had written the text. The text and music first appeared together in 1878 in Ira Sankey's collection *Gospel Hymns No. 3*. The hymn became one of the widely used songs in the great evangelistic crusades of Moody and Sankey, both in this country and throughout Great Britain.

(Instruments begin playing softly)

✳   ✳   ✳   ✳

Reader 1:   How thankful we should be to our Lord that through the years each generation can learn from a choice hymn like this the true meaning of Christ's redemptive love.

Reader 2:   As we sing this hymn today, may these words by Frances Alexander inspire a deeper appreciation within each of us of our Lord's atoning work for our eternal salvation—

Mrs. Alexander: "O DEARLY, DEARLY HAS HE LOVED! AND WE MUST LOVE HIM TOO, AND TRUST IN HIS REDEEMING BLOOD, AND TRY HIS WORKS TO DO."

✳   ✳   ✳   ✳

(Congregation sings "There Is a Green Hill Far Away")

See page 266, *101 Hymn Stories*

Drama 50

This Is My Father's World

3 Characters: 2 Readers, Rev. Maltbie D. Babcock

Reader 1: "The heavens declare the glory of God; the skies proclaim the work of His hands" (Psalm 19:1).

Reader 2: How often we miss much of God's blessing in our lives simply because we fail to take time each day to lift up our eyes and see the glories that our Heavenly Father has created for us to enjoy. Perhaps this is what the Psalmist David meant when he exclaimed in Psalm 121—

Reader 1: "I lift up my eyes to the hills—where does my help come from? My help comes from the Lord, the Maker of heaven and earth" (Psalm 121:1).

Reader 2: Our featured hymnwriter for this service enjoyed frequent early morning walks into the countryside and usually commented . . .

Rev. Maltbie D. Babcock: "I'm going out to see my Father's world."

Reader 1: Written in the year 1900, this is another favorite hymn that is still enjoyed by youth and adults alike—

(Instruments play a portion of "This Is My Father's World")

Reader 1: "This Is My Father's World" was written by a prominent Presbyterian minister, Maltbie D. Babcock. The hymn is taken from his 16-verse poem that was published in 1901 by his wife shortly after her husband's death at the early age of 43.

Reader 2: It was while pastoring in Lockport, New York, that Rev. Babcock would take his morning walks to the top of a nearby hill where he had a full view of Lake Ontario and the beautiful surrounding countryside. There he would listen to the carols of the birds, meditate, commune with his Creator, and simply enjoy the beauties of his Father's world.

Reader 1: Though known for his love of nature and beauty, Rev. Babcock was truly a man's man. It was often said that a more masculine minister never stood in a Christian pulpit. He was tall and broad shouldered with muscles of iron. He was a star baseball player and swimmer. The boys and young men of his community greatly admired him for his athletic abilities yet highly respected him for his strong convictions and Christian principles.

Reader 2:   Something of the dynamic character of Rev. Babcock, both as a man and preacher, is reflected in one of his other well-known poems, "Be Strong."

Rev. Maltbie D. Babcock:

"Be Strong!
We are not here to play, to dream, to drift,
We have hard work to do, and loads to lift.
Shun not the struggle, face it—
'Tis God's gift.

Be Strong!

It matters not how deep entrenched the wrong,
How hard the battle goes, the day how long;
Faint not—fight on! Tomorrow comes the song.

Be Strong!"

(Instruments begin playing softly)

✳ ✳ ✳ ✳

Reader 1:   Throughout the various seasons of the year, there are those times when we are especially awed by some sight of nature—the fresh green buds and flowers of spring, a mountain peak, a beautiful lake or waterfall, or the lovely rich hues of a setting sun. How important it is that Christians live with this kind of sensitive awareness of our Father's world.

Reader 2:   The secret of this awareness is to develop "listening ears" and "seeing eyes." Often it is just the little things in life and nature that provide us with new pleasures—an unusual cloud formation, the singing of a bird, the scent of a flower, the grasp of a friend. Any of these experiences can fill with joy and excite-

ment the life of an individual whose God-given per-
ceptions are truly alive.

Reader 1:   And of all people, Christians should be the most
appreciative of God's created world and keenly desir-
ous of being responsible caretakers of all that is ours to
enjoy in nature.

Reader 2:   May the singing of this hymn encourage us to say
with Maltbie Babcock as we begin each new day—

Rev. Maltbie D. Babcock: "I'm going out to see my Father's
world!"

*   *   *   *

(Congregation sings "This Is My Father's World")

See page 269, *101 Hymn Stories*

- "Nature is like an outstretched finger pointing up
toward heaven."   —Author unknown

- "I cannot conceive how a man could look up into the
heavens and say there is no God."

—Abraham Lincoln

What a Friend We Have in Jesus

3 Characters: 2 Readers, Joseph Scriven

Reader 1: "Do not be anxious about anything, but in everything, by prayer and petition, with thanksgiving, present your requests to God. And the peace of God, which transcends all understanding, will guard your hearts and your minds in Christ Jesus" (Philippians 4:6, 7).

Reader 2: Our featured hymn for this service was written for the purpose of bringing comfort to just one person; yet it has ministered encouragement to countless numbers of Christians since it was first written in the year 1857. In times of stress and grief it reminds us so clearly that we have a heavenly Friend who knows our every weakness and is only a prayer away. The very simplicity of this text and music has been its strong appeal.

(Instruments play a portion of "What a Friend We Have in Jesus")

Reader 2: Regarded as a favorite hymn by many, "What a Friend We Have in Jesus" was written by a very unusual and remarkable man named Joseph Scriven.

Reader 1: Scriven was born of prosperous parents in Dublin, Ireland, in 1820. Later he was graduated from the well-known Trinity College of Dublin. Then at the age of 25, Scriven suddenly decided to leave his native Ireland and migrate to Canada.

Reader 2: His reasons for leaving his family and country seem to have been twofold: The spiritual influence of the Plymouth Brethren upon his life, which estranged him from his family; and the tragic death of his financée by accidental drowning on the evening just before their scheduled wedding.

Reader 1: Upon arriving in Port Hope, Canada, Joseph Scriven began a totally different way of life. As the local school teacher and tutor he gave himself completely to his students and community. He took the Sermon on the

Mount literally as his lifestyle. It is said that he gave freely of his limited possessions, even sharing the clothing from his own body, and never once refused help to anyone who needed it. He became known as the "Good Samaritan" throughout the surrounding area of Port Hope.

Reader 2: One time a prosperous stranger who had arrived in town saw Scriven with his axe and saw in the streets of Port Hope. He asked, "Who is that man? I want him to work for me."

Reader 1: "You cannot get that man . . . he saws wood and works only for poor widows and sick people who cannot pay."

Reader 2: Young Scriven was highly respected but often regarded as rather eccentric by his many neighbors and friends.

Reader 1: "What a Friend We Have in Jesus" was never intended by Scriven for publication. Ten years after he had said goodbye to his mother in Ireland, word came that she was seriously ill. Unable to return to his native homeland, Scriven wrote a letter of comfort to his mother and enclosed the words of his newly written poem with the prayer that these brief lines would always remind her of a never-failing Heavenly Friend.

Reader 2: Sometime later when Joseph Scriven himself was seriously ill, a friend who came to visit him chanced to see a copy of the poem scribbled on scratch paper near his bedside. The friend read the lines with interest . . .

Reader 1: "What a Friend we have in Jesus, all our sins and griefs to bear!
What a privilege to carry everything to God in prayer."

Reader 2: "My, those are interesting lines, Joseph. Who wrote those beautiful words?"

Joseph Scriven: "The Lord and I did it between us."

Reader 1: After the death of Joseph Scriven at the age of 66, which like his fiancée's death also occurred by accidental drowning, the citizens of Port Hope erected a monument which may still be seen today. It was placed there in memory of the man who not only wrote about a Divine Friend but who himself became a daily friend to others.

The entire hymn text is inscribed on the monument with these words . . .

Reader 2: "Four miles north in Pengally's (Pen-GAL-lie's) Cemetery lies the philanthropist and author of this great masterpiece, written at Port Hope, 1857."

Reader 1: The composer of the music for "What a Friend We Have in Jesus" was an American, Charles C. Converse, a noted scholar and an affluent Christian, whose talents ranged from law to professional music.

Reader 2: Though Converse was a highly recognized composer with many of his works performed by the leading American orchestras and choirs of his day, he is best remembered for this simple but tuneful music so well suited to Joseph Scriven's text.

Reader 1: Ira Sankey discovered the hymn in 1875, just in time to include it in his well-known collection, *Sankey's Gospel Hymns Number One.* Later Sankey wrote, "The last hymn which went into the book became one of the first in favor."

(Instruments begin playing softly)

* * * *

Reader 2: As we sing this hymn, may we realize more fully the solemn truth of these challenging words by Joseph Scriven . . .

Joseph Scriven: "O what peace we often forfeit, O what needless pain we bear,
All because we do not carry everything to God in prayer."

Reader 1: But this hymn also assures us that God has made a provision for our every need—

Reader 2: A faithful heavenly Friend—One who "knows our every weakness, who will all our sorrows share."

Joseph Scriven: "In His arms He'll take and shield thee—Thou wilt find a solace (SOL-is) there."

* * * *

(Congregation sings "What a Friend We Have in Jesus")

See page 275, *101 Hymn Stories*

Drama 52

Wonderful Grace of Jesus

3 Characters: 2 Readers, Haldor Lillenas

Reader 1: "For you know the grace of our Lord Jesus Christ, that though He was rich, yet for your sakes He became poor, so that you through His poverty might become rich" (2 Corinthians 8:9).

Reader 2: Through the years Christian leaders have been much impressed with the marvel and mystery of God's grace—the unmerited favor of a holy God in providing redemption for a depraved human race. And truly any sincere believer must stand in awe, as did the author of this hymn, with the scope of divine provision for man's sin—

Haldor Lillenas: * "Deeper than the mighty rolling sea," "higher than the mountain," "greater far than all my sin and shame."

(Instruments play a portion of the chorus of "Wonderful Grace of Jesus")

Reader 2: "Wonderful Grace of Jesus" was written in the year 1918 by one of the leading twentieth century American hymn writers, Haldor Lillenas.

Reader 1: Haldor Lillenas was born in 1885 in the beautiful fjord (fi-ORD) country of Norway. He came to the United States as a child and lived with his family in South Dakota and later in Oregon.

Reader 2: Through the ministry of the City Rescue Mission in Portland, Oregon, Haldor Lillenas had a dramatic conversion experience when he was 21 years of age. He soon felt the call from God to preach the gospel and to write songs that would reach the hearts of people.

Reader 1: He attended Pasadena College in Los Angeles and then married Bertha Mae Wilson, a noted song writer and musician. Mr. and Mrs. Lillenas became active in the leadership of Nazarene churches.

Reader 2:   Then for some time Mr. and Mrs. Lillenas traveled extensively throughout this country, conducting evangelistic meetings as well as furnishing songs and choir music for many leading song leaders such as Charles Alexander and Homer Hammontree. During this period Mr. Lillenas also served short pastorates in various Nazarene churches in California, Texas, Indiana, and Illinois.

Reader 1:   It was while pastoring in Illinois that Haldor Lillenas wrote "Wonderful Grace of Jesus."

Haldor Lillenas: "In 1917 Mrs. Lillenas and I built our first home in the town of Olivet, Illinois. Upon its completion, we had scarcely any money left to furnish the little house. Having no piano at the time, and needing an instrument of some kind, I managed to find, at one of the neighbor's homes, a little wheezy organ which I purchased for $5.00. With the aid of this instrument, a number of my songs were written which are now popular, including 'Wonderful Grace of Jesus.' It was sung by the great chorus in 1918 at the Northfield Massachusetts Bible Conference, being introduced for the first time by Homer Hammontree."

Reader 2:   "Wonderful Grace of Jesus" was first published in the *Tabernacle Choir Book Collection*, for which Mr. Lillenas was paid the grand sum of $5.00.

Reader 1:   Soon, however, this $5.00 song composed on a $5.00 wheezy organ became popular world-wide as a stirring mass choir selection for the city-wide evangelistic crusades of that time. And still today, seldom can a song leader ask any group of believers for their choice of a hymn without someone in the congregation requesting this inspiring favorite.

Reader 2:   Although we generally like to sing this hymn with a rather brisk tempo, Mr. Lillenas often complained that in most congregations the hymn was sung too fast.

Haldor Lillenas: "A song should be performed in such a fashion that the words can be comfortably pronounced and understood without undue haste."

Reader 1:   Haldor Lillenas wrote approximately 4,000 gospel hymn texts and tunes. In addition to "Wonderful

Grace of Jesus," some of his songs still frequently sung are—

Reader 2:   "The Bible Stands Like a Rock Undaunted"; "It Is Glory Just to Walk with Him"; "Jesus Has Lifted Me"; "Peace, Peace, Wonderful Peace"; and "My Wonderful Lord."

Reader 1:   In 1924 Mr. Lillenas founded the Lillenas Music Company, which merged several years later with the Nazarene Publishing Company. He remained with this company as its music editor for the next 20 years.

Reader 2:   Before his home-going at Aspen, Colorado in 1959 at the age of 74, Lillenas was recognized for his many contributions to the Christian ministry and was awarded an honorary Doctor of Music degree from Olivet Nazarene College of Kankakee, Illinois.

(Instruments begin playing softly)

* * * *

Reader 1:   How important it is that we realize with conviction that it is the free gift of grace that assures our eternal standing with God—nothing we can do, feel, or earn. We must simply receive by faith this divine gift purchased for us on Calvary's cross.

Reader 2:   And the grace that provided our salvation is also available for our daily living. The writer of the book of Hebrews encourages us to "approach the throne of grace with confidence, so that we may receive mercy . . .

Reader 1:   AND FIND GRACE TO HELP IN TIME OF NEED" (Hebrews 4:16).

Reader 2:   As we sing this inspiring hymn, may these words by Haldor Lillenas be the joyous response from each of our hearts for God's wonderful gift of grace—

Haldor Lillenas: "O MAGNIFY THE PRECIOUS NAME OF JESUS, PRAISE HIS NAME!"

* * * *

(Congregation sings "Wonderful Grace of Jesus")

See page 314, *101 More Hymn Stories*

Other Music Resources by Kenneth W. Osbeck

Amazing Grace: *366 Hymn Stories for Personal Devotions*
An inspirational daily devotional based on 366 great hymns of the Christian faith. Each day's devotional highlights biblical truths drawn from the true-to-life experiences behind the writing of these well-known hymns. Each story contains a portion of the hymn itself, as well as suggested Scripture readings, meditations, and practical applications. Your personal or family devotional time will be enhanced by the challenging and inspiring thoughts contained in this thrilling collection of classical and contemporary hymn stories.
ISBN 0-8254-3425-4   384 pp.   paperback

Devotional Warm-ups for the Church Choir
A variety of 43 brief, challenging devotionals on 10 different musically oriented topics. Designed to provide spiritually stimulating material for church choir members, both individually and as a group. Pertinent group discussion questions as well as accompanying Scripture reflections are provided for each study.
ISBN 0-8254-3421-1   96 pp.   paperback

Junior's Praise
100 selected hymns specifically designed to meet the needs of evangelical churches in teaching boys and girls, ages 7 to 12, the standard hymns of the faith.
ISBN 0-8254-3400-9   174 pp.   paperback

My Music Workbook
A book devoted to bringing a basic understanding of music to Junior Age children. Excellent as a textbook for Christian schools and graded church choirs.
ISBN 0-8254-3415-7   144 pp.   paperback

The Ministry of Music

A practical handbook on music and its application in the local church ministry. Widely used as a textbook in Bible schools.

ISBN 0-8254-3410-6   192 pp.   paperback

101 Hymn Stories

(Foreword by J. Stratton Shufelt.) The true-life experiences and inspirational background stories behind 101 favorite hymns. Excellent for devotional reading, sermon illustrations, and bulletin inserts, as well as for historical or biographical research. Includes the complete hymn with each story.

ISBN 0-8254-3416-5   288 pp.   paperback

101 More Hymn Stories

(Foreword by Cliff Barrows.) The stories behind the hymns of 101 additional past and contemporary favorites with the music included. An important companion volume to *101 Hymn Stories.*

ISBN 0-8254-3420-3   328 pp.   paperback

Pocket Guide for the Church Choir Member

A helpful sourcebook of the fundamentals of musical knowledge designed to make every choir member effective. Contains a useful glossary of key musical terms.

ISBN 0-8254-3408-4   48 pp.   paperback

Available at your Christian bookstore, or

P. O. Box 2607 • Grand Rapids, MI 49501